The
Love
That
Dares

The Love That Dares

Letters of LGBTQ+ Love & Friendship Through History

ilex

Rachel Smith & Barbara Vesey

Foreword by **Mark Gatiss**

For Hannah and Joe and Paul, of course
– B.V.

For Katrina – for everything
– R.S.

Contents

Foreword

The age of the letter, it is popularly supposed, is dead. Yet what this charming, moving and fascinating collection proves is that the form itself – a scribbled note, a declaration of love, an outpouring of passion, a bitter word – has always been with us. We begin with Lord Alfred Douglas's notorious poem 'Two Loves', used as evidence to crucify Oscar Wilde and provoking his famous, if disingenuous defence of the love that had existed between the biblical David and Jonathan. But that's merely the scene-setter for a very diverse archive of the LGBTQ experience.

It's wonderful to actually read some of Sappho – a poet who feels mythical by dint of being, as it were, the original Lesbian. Yet here she is, emerging from legend as a very real person, burning for another woman – 'subtly under my skin runs a fire ecstatic' – articulating the ageless sense of pulse-quickening desire.

Here, too, are the lines of the young Marcus Aurelius to his teacher, as sweet and gushing as any teenager's agonized note: 'Farewell, breath of my life. Should I not burn with love of you, who have written to me as you have! What shall I do? I cannot cease.'

Secrecy, of course, is a constant theme. I can remember calling my own first boyfriend on the phone during the summer holidays and having an agonizingly stiff conversation with him. I was convinced he no longer cared and poured out my feelings in a tortured scrawl, only to receive a hugely apologetic note in the big looped fountain-penned hand which I'd come to adore, explaining that he'd been unable to talk openly. There are more 'emotionally-restricted telephone talks' in Benjamin Britten's letters to Peter Pears. They have the wonderful familiarity of a couple's life, with Britten addressing Pears as 'my little pussy cat', speaking of weeping at the movies and 'every loving couple I see I envy'.

And there's Anne Lister, made famous now as 'Gentleman Jack', and her lover Ann Walker warning, 'Read this alone'. Who knows how many coded, ecstatic little messages have been lost to us, burned by embarrassed family members or to head off police searches?

But not all is wistful, reserved and sad. There's a joyous liberation in John Cage starkly admitting to his lover: 'Starved for good long fuck with you'!

For a community which has lived too long with shame and oppression, this is a wonderful snapshot of a timeless and continuing presence. From ancient texts to Instagram posts, we are here and have always been here with the same current of desires, thwarted loves, pain and pleasure resonating throughout.

Mark Gatiss

Epigraph

Two Loves

I dreamed I stood upon a little hill,
And at my feet there lay a ground, that seemed
Like a waste garden, flowering at its will
With buds and blossoms. There were pools that dreamed
Black and unruffled; there were white lilies
A few, and crocuses, and violets
Purple or pale, snake-like fritillaries
Scarce seen for the rank grass, and through green nets
Blue eyes of shy peryenche winked in the sun.
And there were curious flowers, before unknown,
Flowers that were stained with moonlight, or with shades
Of Nature's willfull moods; and here a one
That had drunk in the transitory tone
Of one brief moment in a sunset; blades
Of grass that in an hundred springs had been
Slowly but exquisitely nurtured by the stars,
And watered with the scented dew long cupped

The Love That Dares

In lilies, that for rays of sun had seen
Only God's glory, for never a sunrise mars
The luminous air of Heaven. Beyond, abrupt,
A grey stone wall o'ergrown with velvet moss
Uprose; and gazing I stood long, all mazed
To see a place so strange, so sweet, so fair.
And as I stood and marvelled, lo! across
The garden came a youth; one hand he raised
To shield him from the sun, his wind-tossed hair
Was twined with flowers, and in his hand he bore
A purple bunch of bursting grapes, his eyes
Were clear as crystal, naked all was he,
White as the snow on pathless mountains frore,
Red were his lips as red wine-spilith that dyes
A marble floor, his brow chalcedony.
And he came near me, with his lips uncurled
And kind, and caught my hand and kissed my mouth,
And gave me grapes to eat, and said, 'Sweet friend,
Come I will show thee shadows of the world
And images of life. See from the South
Comes the pale pageant that hath never an end.'
And lo! within the garden of my dream
I saw two walking on a shining plain
Of golden light. The one did joyous seem
And fair and blooming, and a sweet refrain

Came from his lips; he sang of pretty maids
And joyous love of comely girl and boy,
His eyes were bright, and 'mid the dancing blades
Of golden grass his feet did trip for joy;
And in his hand he held an ivory lute
With strings of gold that were as maidens' hair,
And sang with voice as tuneful as a flute,
And round his neck three chains of roses were.
But he that was his comrade walked aside;
He was full sad and sweet, and his large eyes
Were strange with wondrous brightness, staring wide
With gazing; and he sighed with many sighs
That moved me, and his cheeks were wan and white
Like pallid lilies, and his lips were red
Like poppies, and his hands he clenched tight,
And yet again unclenched, and his head
Was wreathed with moon flowers pale as lips of death.
A purple robe he wore, o'erwrought in gold
With the device of a great snake, whose breath
Was fiery flame: which when I did behold
I fell a-weeping, and I cried, 'Sweet youth,
Tell me why, sad and sighing, thou dost rove
These pleasant realms? I pray thee speak me sooth
What is thy name?' He said, 'My name is Love.'
Then straight the first did turn himself to me

The Love That Dares

And cried, 'He lieth, for his name is Shame,
But I am Love, and I was wont to be
Alone in this fair garden, till he came
Unasked by night; I am true Love, I fill
The hearts of boy and girl with mutual flame.'
Then sighing, said the other, 'Have thy will,
I am the love that dare not speak its name.'

– Lord Alfred Douglas, 1892

Introduction

This project started when our editor at Ilex got in touch with Stef Dickers, our boss and Special Collections and Archives Manager at Bishopsgate Institute, London. The materials we look after reflect LGBTQ+ experiences in the UK and around the world, and include thousands of books, journals, magazines, pamphlets, zines, press cuttings, photographs, posters, placards, badges, T-shirts, dresses, leather gear, brochures, postcards, sex toys, club flyers and health leaflets, from organizations such as Switchboard, Stonewall, Terrence Higgins Trust, Gay Men Fighting AIDS, Rebel Dykes, the Museum of Transology, London Gay Men's Chorus, Outrage! and UK Leather Archive as well as from individuals such as Sue Sanders, Peter Tatchell, Paris Lees and Sarah Jane Baker. Ellie approached Stef, knowing about the Institute's reputation as one of the major repositories of material relating to the history and future of LGBTQ+ life in the UK, and asked him if he would like the opportunity to bring this material to a wider audience. Stef, in turn, asked us if we'd like to take up the challenge. The result is this book.

This is an eclectic selection, by no means definitive. We realized immediately that any attempt to be comprehensive would always fall short. There have been millions of LGBTQ+ letters and letter-writers throughout history, and there was no way we could do justice to even a fraction of them. We have chosen the letters we came across in the course of our research that we've found delightful, moving and, in our opinion, important.

As we started to research, we based our choices on, first, wanting to give some kind of historical overview. Today, even with all our relative sophistication and knowledge of gay history, it is still important to highlight that there have always been queer people. So this collection includes letters from *c.*590 BCE right up to 2021. The order is mainly chronological, but in places we have grouped letters together by theme instead where this felt more logical and appropriate. We have also tried to let the letters speak for themselves, where possible, but have provided biographical information and context where this seemed necessary. Where the original source provided fuller information about dates, places and other background information, we have included it.

Secondly, we tried hard not to include only writers – though obviously it tends to be writers, whether of poetry, fiction, prose or political tracts, whose letters get saved and published. For this reason we have perhaps left out some better-known names in favour of musicians, artists, composers, activists, teachers and 'unfamous' folk whose letters of love and friendship have found their way into the collections we hold at Bishopsgate Institute, or which have been published by those who have felt, as we do, that making these individuals better known is a more accurate way of reflecting the LGBTQ+ community.

This collection stretches the 'letter' genre to include poetry and a note scribbled by a man to his partner as he was rushing off to work. There are letters from one person to an unknown other and letters between two lovers or friends. Then there are letters expressing gratitude to a person (or, in one instance, a magazine) for their very existence, for forging the way ahead and demonstrating a way of being, of living, that helped the letter-writer know and celebrate themselves. Examples of this last type of letter include Siegfried Sassoon's (frankly fan-boy) letter to Edward Carpenter, Lorraine Hansberry's letter to the lesbian magazine *The Ladder* and MC Sherman's letters during the 2020 US presidential campaign about their hopes and fears for the future.

Letters are, of course, very personal and normally private – one reason why it's such a privilege to be able to have this glimpse into people's lives. LGBTQ+ letters are, if anything, more private, more hidden than those of heterosexual and cisgender people because of the added layer of secrecy brought about by fear of reprisal, hatred or criminal punishment. Because of these inherent dangers – sadly still with us even today – and for other, happier reasons (writers working on books of their own, for example), it has sometimes proved difficult for us to secure permission to reprint letters we would have loved to include. When this happened (and we were given the person's OK), we have included them in the References and Resources section, so you can explore them and their work for yourself. Where letters (originals or earlier published versions) are held at Bishopsgate Institute, we have indicated this – and everyone is welcome to come and look at them whenever they wish.

Finally, we want to extend an invitation: if you have letters of your own, or ones that have been sent to you, that you would like to donate to Bishopsgate Institute, we would be thrilled to have them. We will look after them in perpetuity and make them accessible to researchers based on your preferences, keeping them open or closed (inaccessible to the public) for as long as you request, to protect any living persons or yourself until such time as the danger of any hurt or harm being caused has passed. If you would like more information on how to contribute your letters to the archive at Bishopsgate, turn to the back of the book (page 259).

– Barbara Vesey

First, a few words about language. LGBTQ+ people have always been part of human history, but the language used to describe the LGBTQ+ experience has not always existed or been consistent, and it is still evolving. So when speaking (writing) about LGBTQ+ people from the past, we must exercise caution lest we project backwards and assign modern customs and ideas anachronistically. In this book we have tried to provide historical context to illuminate the moments in time which produced these letters and the people who wrote them. This will include how these people were described while they were alive, by themselves and others, and will also include how we might describe them today.

On a more practical note, some of the letter writers included could not spell for toffee and had only a perfunctory grasp of grammar. We have tried to keep their original spellings, syntax and so on, in the interests of being true to them. In the one or two cases where this would have actually impeded comprehension, we have indicated that we have cleaned up the spelling a bit.

Just as LGBTQ+ love should be celebrated as much as heterosexual love, so too we should recognize that queer people are as imperfect as straight people. That is to say, some of the letter-writers included in this book were at times of questionable character. The ethos of this project is very much to let the letters speak for themselves, and so when providing context for them we will hold a mirror up to who the writers were, flaws and all.

In *Nineteen Eighty-Four* George Orwell wrote, 'Who controls the past controls the future: who controls the present controls the past.' While homosexuality, bisexuality, gender nonconformity and being transgender are as natural as human nature itself, LGBTQ+ people have experienced and are still experiencing marginalization and suffering, up to and including death. LGBTQ+ folk have been reduced to the margins, and within those margins lie intersecting subsets of further marginalization. Therefore, when compiling these letters we consciously wanted to feature not just well-known names from history, but also 'everyday' people and their experiences.

The phrase 'the love that dare not speak its name' comes from a poem written by Lord Alfred Douglas (we've included it in its entirety in the Epigraph). Douglas is better known by his nickname 'Bosie' and for having been Oscar Wilde's lover (and the means of his eventual downfall and imprisonment). This love letter of sorts was read aloud as criminal evidence during Wilde's libel case against Douglas's father at the Old Bailey in 1895. John Douglas, the Marquess of Queensberry, had accused Wilde in writing of being a 'somdomite' (*sic*). In response to the question, 'What is the "love that dare not speak its name"?' Wilde replied in court:

> The love that dare not speak its name in this century is such a great affection of an elder for a younger man as there was between David and Jonathan, such as Plato made the very basis of his philosophy, and such as you find in the sonnets of Michelangelo and Shakespeare. It is that deep, spiritual affection that is as pure as it is perfect. It dictates and pervades great works of art like those of Shakespeare and Michelangelo, and those two letters of mine, such as they are. It is in this century misunderstood, so much misunderstood that it may be described as the Love that dare not speak its name, and on account of it I am placed where I am now. It is beautiful, it is fine, it is the noblest form of affection. There is nothing unnatural about it. It is intellectual, and it repeatedly exists between an elder and a younger man, when the elder man has intellect, and the younger man has all the joy, hope and glamour of life before him. That it should be so the world does not understand. The world mocks at it and sometimes puts one in the pillory for it.

Many years later, in 1976, the phrase was paraphrased in the title of a poem written by James Kirkup, 'The Love That Dares to Speak Its Name'. The persona of the poem is a Roman centurion who after the Crucifixion has sex (described in some detail – definitely NSFW!) with the recently deceased Jesus Christ. The poem was published in *Gay News*, which was then sued for blasphemy by the conservative activist Mary Whitehouse. Whitehouse won the court case and later received a CBE. It is still to this day technically illegal to publish the poem. Several of the letters in this book could have landed their writers in prison if found by the wrong people; if written today in certain countries, they would be considered criminal. Others were written against a backdrop of state vilification during Section 28 in the UK, 'Don't Ask, Don't Tell' in the US and the HIV/AIDS epidemic. It is important to remember the love LGBTQ+ people have shared as well as the struggles they have endured, just as it is important to remember the battles we have won and lost; to remember how far we have come and to be vigilant about never going back, and to love one another and ourselves regardless. And so, the true 'love that dares' is one that will never remain silent; one that loves unashamedly – proudly.

– Rachel Smith

The
Letters

Sappho
(c.620–570 BCE)

We start not with letters as such but with poetry – all we have of the mystery who was Sappho. Even her poetry collections are fragmented. She was born on the Greek island of Lesbos – therefore, she was a Lesbian. She was known as 'The Poetess' in the same way Homer was referred to as 'The Poet' and her work was often in tribute to Aphrodite, goddess of beauty and youth. Sappho also describes her passionate love of women, including Anactoria, who is the subject of the poems included here. It is this passion which later led some to describe love between women as sapphic.

Anacreon's Song

Golden-throned Muse, sing the song that in olden
Days was sung of love and delight in Teos,
In the goodly land of the lovely women:
Strains that in other

Years the hoary bard with the youthful fancy
Set to mirthful stir of flutes, when the dancing
Nymphs that poured the wine for the poet's banquet
Mixed it with kisses;

Sing the song while I, in the arms of Atthis,
Seal her lips to mine with a lover's fervour,
Breathe her breath and drink her sighs to the honeyed
Lull of the melics.

Moon and Stars

When the moon at full on the sill of heaven
Lights her beacon, flooding the earth with silver,
All the shining stars that about her cluster
Hide their fair faces;

So when Anactoria's beauty dazzles
Sight of mine, grown dim with the joy it gives me,

Gorgo, Atthis, Gyrinno, all the others
Fade from my vision.

Ode to Anactoria

Peer of Gods to me is the man thy presence
Crowns with joy; who hears, as he sits beside thee,
Accents sweet of thy lips the silence breaking,
With lovely laughter;

Tones that make the heart in my bosom flutter,
For if I, the space of a moment even,
Near to thee come, any word I would utter
Instantly fails me;

Vain my stricken tongue would a whisper fashion,
Subtly under my skin runs fire ecstatic;
Straightway mists surge dim to my eyes and leave them
Reft of their vision;

Echoes ring in my ears; a trembling seizes
All my body bathed in soft perspiration;
Pale as grass I grow in my passion's madness,
Like one insensate;

But must I dare all, since to me unworthy,
Bliss thy beauty brings that a God might envy;
Never yet was fervid woman a fairer
Image of Kypris.

Ah! undying Daughter of God, befriend me!
Calm my blood that thrills with impending transport;
Feed my lips the murmur of words to stir her
Bosom to pity;

Overcome with kisses her faintest protest,
Melt her mood to mine with amorous touches,
Till her low assent and her sigh's abandon
Lure me to rapture.

Marcus Aurelius
(121–180 CE)

Marcus Aurelius was a Roman emperor, philosopher and diarist, widely known today for his work *Meditations*, exploring his Stoic philosophy. Before all of that, he was a young student when, in 139 CE, Marcus Cornelius Fronto was selected to instruct him in rhetoric. Marcus Aurelius, just eighteen at the time, was infatuated from the start and was soon referring to his teacher as 'my Fronto', 'my number one delight', 'my dearest and most loving', 'my biggest thing under heaven' and 'breath of my life'.

In ancient Rome, romantic love between men was viewed as a crime only if an older man seduced a young boy. There is no evidence as to whether the two Marcuses ever became more than student and teacher, but from the letters included here, it is clear that Marcus Aurelius loved Marcus Cornelius Fronto passionately.

Hail, my best of masters.

Go on, threaten me as much as you please and
attack me with hosts of arguments, yet shall you
never drive your lover, I mean me, away; nor shall
I the less assert that I love Fronto, or love him the
less, because you prove with reasons so various and
so vehement that those who are less in love must
be more helped and indulged. So passionately, by
Hercules, am I in love with you, nor am I frightened
off by the law you lay down, and even if you show
yourself more forward and facile to others, who are
non-lovers, yet will I love you while I have life and
health ...

This I can without rashness affirm: if that
Phaedrus of yours ever really existed, if he was ever
away from Socrates, Socrates never felt for Phaedrus
a more passionate longing than I for the sight of
you all these days: days do I say? months I mean
... unless he is straightway seized with love of you.
Farewell, my greatest treasure beneath the sky, my
glory. It is enough to have had such a master. My
Lady mother sends you greeting.

Hail, my best of masters.

If any sleep comes back to you after the wakeful
nights of which you complain, I beseech you write
to me and, above all, I beseech you take care of your
health. Then hide somewhere and bury that 'axe
of Tenedos', which you hold over us, and do not,
whatever you do, give up your intention of pleading
cases, or along with yours let all lips be dumb …

  Farewell, breath of my life. Should I not burn
with love of you, who have written to me as you
have! What shall I do? I cannot cease. Last year it
befell me in this very place, and at this very time,
to be consumed with a passionate longing for my
mother. This year you inflame that my longing.
My Lady greets you.

St Anselm
(1033–1109)

Born in Aosta, Italy, the theologian and cleric Anselm became a Benedictine monk at Bec Abbey in Normandy at the age of twenty-three. He went on to become a prior at thirty, an abbot at forty-five and the archbishop of Canterbury at sixty. He was canonized as a Catholic saint in 1163.

In true repressed fashion, these letters to his fellow monk Brother Gilbert Crispin are unrequited love personified: all frustration, passion and unfulfilled longing. Like the ancient Greeks before him, Anselm felt deeply for his students, often addressing them as a 'beloved lover' (*dilecto dilectori*). We can't know if Anselm ever physically acted upon his feelings, but as any LGBTQ+ person can tell you, one's sexuality need not be manifested in the flesh to be any less real.

Anselm very well may have been merely acting as modern-day Catholicism dictates: love the sinner, hate the sin. He laid the framework for this rhetoric in his response to the Council of London in 1102, where the church wanted to declare sodomy a sin for the first time in English ecclesiastical history.

At this time Anselm, as archbishop of Canterbury, told the Council they were better off not enacting this legislation because homosexual and bisexual men were so 'widespread' across the country, and so few of them were even 'embarrassed by [being gay] or had even been aware it was a serious matter'.

Anselm agreed that known homosexual or bisexual men should not be admitted to the priesthood, but said that, when hearing confessions of sins of the same flesh, priests 'should take into account mitigating factors such as age and marital status before prescribing penance', and he advised counselling rather than punishment.

Brother Anselm to his master, brother, friend,
Gilbert: the friend of his beloved one: that which
writing cannot express. Sweet are to me, dearest
friend, the proofs of thy affection: but they can in
nowise relieve my heart, deprived of thee, from the
longing for thy beloved self. Assuredly, wert thou
to send every aromatic scent, all glittering metals,
every precious stone, all kinds of woven beauty, it
would reject them; nay, my heart could never be
healed of its wound but by receiving the other half
of itself which has been torn away from it. Witness
the grief of my heart when thinking thereon; the
tears which dim my eyes and fall down my face and
on my fingers as I write. And indeed thou knowest
as myself my love towards thee, but certainly I
was ignorant of it. He who separated us from one
another, He has taught me how much I loved thee:
truly that man has no knowledge of good or evil
who does not experience both. For never having
made trial of thine absence I was unaware how
sweet it was to me to be with, and how bitter to be
without, thee. But thou hast in consequence of our
separation another present with thee whom thou

lovest not less, but more; whilst thou art removed, thou I say from me art removed, and no one is given me in thy place. Since, then, thou art rejoicing in thy consolation, for the wound is gaping in my soul only, perchance they who are enjoying thy society are offended at my saying this to thee. But if they rejoice while keeping that which they wished for, why should they forbid him to lament who has not that which still he loves. They will excuse me, seeing me in themselves. Moreover can you understand how compassionately, how feelingly they can do this, and whence my grief can be lessened, which no one will console who can, and no one can who would. But may He who can do all that He wills, so comfort me as that He may sadden no one; so may He sadden no one, as that He may preserve for thee the love everywhere felt, unimpaired.

James I
(1566–1625)

The son of Mary, Queen of Scots, James Charles Stuart was James VI of Scotland from 1567 and succeeded his mother's cousin Elizabeth I to the English throne in 1603.

A few decades before James was born, Henry VIII and his government passed the Buggery Act in 1533, which for over 300 years carried a death sentence by hanging for all men who were found to have had sex with other men. Prior to this legislation, the fate of men who loved men was in the hands of the Catholic Church and its laws and courts. The Buggery Act was passed shortly before the First Act of Succession, which declared Henry VIII's marriage to Catherine of Aragon null and void, and thereby paved the way not only for Henry to marry Anne Boleyn, but also for the birth of the Church of England.

The Buggery Act was repealed by Mary I (1516–58) because of her allegiance to the Catholic Church, then reinstated by Elizabeth I (1533–1603) because of her allegiance to the Church of England.

Under a new name (The Offences Against the Person Act of 1828), sexual love between two men was a capital crime – punishable by death – until well into Queen Victoria's reign. Though the Sexual Offences Act of 1967 saw the partial decriminalization of sexual acts between men aged over twenty-one in England and Wales, throughout what was still the British Empire homosexuality remained a criminal offence. Today, out of fifty-four countries in the Commonwealth, LGBTQ+ people can love legally in only nineteen of them, and face hard labour, corporal punishment and life imprisonment for the 'crime' of loving another person in the remaining thirty-five.

King James publicly declared homosexuality a 'horrible crime' which Christians were morally 'bound' to never forgive. However, privately he was known to have serious and passionate relationships with several male courtiers. Among his many biographers are those who maintain that George Villiers (later Duke of Buckingham), Esmé Stewart (later Duke of Lennox) and Robert Carr (later Earl of Somerset) were among his lovers. Historians have also noted that one of the reasons Shakespeare chose to publish a full collection of his sonnets in 1609, even though he had written many of them some ten years earlier, was that sonnets addressing a beautiful boy (as a lot of the earlier ones do) would be looked upon more favourably in the 'homosocial' court of King James.

The following letters are from King James to George Villiers, or 'Steenie' as James called him, after St Stephen who was said to have an angelic face. As with Marcus Aurelius and Marcus Cornelius Fronto, no one will ever know whether or not James and George consummated their relationship; however, these letters are evidence of the passion between them.

17 May 1620

My only sweet and dear child,

Thy dear dad sends thee his blessing this morning
and also to his daughter. The Lord of Heaven send
you a sweet and blithe wakening, all kind of comfort
in your sanctified bed, and bless the fruits thereof
that I may have sweet bedchamber boys to play me
with, and this is my daily prayer, sweet heart. When
thou risest, keep thee from importunity of people
that may trouble thy mind, that at meeting I may
see thy white teeth shine upon me, and so bear me
comfortable company in my journey. And so God
bless thee, hoping thou will not forget to read over
again my former letter.

James R.

December 1623[?]

My only sweet and dear child,

Notwithstanding of your desiring me not to write yesterday, yet had I written in the evening if, at my coming out of the park, such a drowsiness had not come upon me as I was forced to set and sleep in my chair half an hour. And yet I cannot content myself without sending you this present, praying God that I may have a joyful and comfortable meeting with you and that we may make at this Christmas a new marriage ever to be kept hereafter; for, God so love me, as I desire only to live in this world for your sake, and that I had rather live banished in any part of the earth with you than live a sorrowful widow's life without you. And so God bless you, my sweet child and wife, and grant that ye may ever be a comfort to your dear dad and husband.

James R.

Sonnet LXXX

William Shakespeare was commissioned to write seventeen sonnets by Mary, 2nd Countess of Southampton, in order to encourage her seventeen-year-old son to marry. This was a serious business: the boy was betrothed to the granddaughter of Lord Burghley, Elizabeth I's Secretary of State, and the family would be fined £2.5 million in today's money if the boy shirked his 'duty'.

Shakespeare accepted the commission and composed the initial sonnets, then took so to the poetic form (and, it is said, to the boy) that he wrote more and more (though it is worth noting that the order in which they were published – and the order in which they are presented in every edition we have – is not always the order in which they were written). As a sequence they seem to get more and more personal, more and more passionate.

Sonnet LXXX (that is, number 80 of the 154 we have today) concerns itself not just with the beloved but also with a rival – apparently younger, stronger and more virile than the 'I' of the poem. If you think it sounds a little double entendre-y ('whilst he upon your soundless deep doth ride') you are absolutely right. The final couplet seems, to us and to far wiser scholars than us, to express the beautiful and poignant idea that love is never wasted, even if not reciprocated.

Oh! how I faint when I of you do write,
Knowing a better spirit doth use your name,
And in the praise thereof spends all his might,
To make me tongue-tied speaking of your fame.
But since your worth, wide as the ocean is,
The humble as the proudest sail doth bear,
My saucy bark, inferior far to his,
On your broad main doth wilfully appear.
Your shallowest help will hold me up afloat,
Whilst he upon your soundless deep doth ride,
Or, being wracked, I am a worthless boat,
He of tall building, and of goodly pride:
    Then if he thrive and I be cast away,
    The worst was this, my love was my decay.

Katherine Philips
(1632–1664)

Katherine Philips (née Fowler) was a poet who achieved fame as a translator and woman of letters. Her poems were published after her death. The poets John Dryden and John Keats were among many others who cited her as an influence on their work.

She was married at the age of sixteen, but as this was the 17th century she didn't necessarily have a say in the arrangement. Her poems were always on female friendship, but used the kind of erotic language usually reserved for love poetry. In fact, her poems mention Sappho as a muse and Philips herself has been compared to Sappho. Katherine Philips was herself referred to as 'The Matchless Orinda' (and as this 'Orinda' refers to herself in the poem that follows).

To My Excellent Lucasia, on Our Friendship

I did not live until this time
Crowned my felicity –
When I could say without a crime
I am not thine, but thee.
This carcass breathed, and walked, and slept,
So that the world believed
There was a soul the motions kept;
But they were all deceived.
For as a watch by art is wound
To motion, such was mine:
But never had Orinda found
A soul till she found thine
Which now inspires, cures and supplies,
And guides my darkened breast:
For thou art all that I can prize,
My joy, my life, my rest.
No bridegroom's nor crown-conqueror's mirth
To mine compared can be:
They have but pieces of this earth,
I've all the world in thee.
Then let our flames still light and shine,
And no false fear control,
As innocent as our design,
Immortal as our soul.

Anne Lister
(1791–1840)
&
Ann Walker
(1803–1854)

Anne Lister and Ann Walker, whose love story was celebrated in the BBC TV series *Gentleman Jack*, were partners for six years until Lister's untimely death at the age of forty-nine. A wealthy landowner in Calderdale, West Yorkshire, Lister was rich enough to be able to ignore conventional calls upon her to marry a man and instead to live her life as she chose.

The world learned of Lister's twenty-six volumes of coded diaries detailing her loves and sexual conquests in 1988, when extracts were first compiled for publication by Helena Whitbread, who worked painstakingly to decode the text in Lister's diaries. The code had been deciphered much earlier, in 1933, by a descendant of

Lister's, who was advised to burn the diaries once their content was known. Luckily he refused. In 2011 her diaries were added to the UNESCO Memory of the World Register, for their 'comprehensive and painfully honest account of lesbian life'.

The following letter from Ann Walker was transcribed by Lister into one of her diaries, together with her comments in square brackets. The ring mentioned in the letter refers to an engagement ring, for Lister had told Walker she wanted to marry her. In early 1833 Walker was visiting a relative in Scotland and Lister was in Europe; though they kept in touch through letters, they did not see each other until January 1834 – by February Walker had moved into Shibden Hall, and there she and Lister exchanged rings and vows.

Nov 12 1832

I have received a letter, which you shall see, <u>but we must meet on different terms</u>. Oh that I had taken you at your word last Monday, and as you said finished the matter on that day. I should then have spared you this additional bitterness.

I did hope when my <u>word was once given to you</u> that I should have felt at rest and satisfied, but in reflecting on all you have said and trying to turn it to my own advantage I cannot satisfy my conscience, and with such sufferings as I have endured since Wednesday, I feel I could not make you happy. That I should only bring misery upon you, for misery I am sure it would be to you to see me in the state I have been in for several days.

It was this sort of wretchedness that was expressed in my note on Friday. It was these miserable feelings that prompted my request

[that is I suppose for me not to send to York for the ring]

<u>For your own sake, fly whilst it is yet in your power,</u>

[I smile as I copy this sentence]

and believe that I will never intrude myself in any way upon you (unless it is your wish) whenever you revisit the neighbourhood.

Nov[embe]r 12 eighteen hundred and 32

[written on the outside of this half sheet but under cover,]

<u>Read this alone</u>

The Ladies of Llangollen

Eleanor Butler (1739–1829) and Sarah Ponsonby (1755–1831) were members of the Irish aristocracy who first met in 1768. They escaped the social confines of Ireland (then still part of the UK) in 1778 for the relative anonymity and freedom of North Wales, taking up residence in a small cottage which they proceeded to beautify and expand. Coming to be known as 'The Ladies of Llangollen', they lived together for fifty years, receiving many guests, including literary giants of the time such as Robert Southey, Anna Seward, Sir Walter Scott and Caroline Lamb, and also Anne Lister, who, some scholars believe, was inspired by them to informally marry her own lover. Extant letters are scarce (the two were rarely apart), but in her book about the pair Elizabeth Mavor notes that they would often spend up to six hours a day on their correspondence, and that 'Each was mistress of the contents of the other's letters, frequently they wrote as one.'

George Sand
(1804–1876)

In a letter to the novelist Honoré de Balzac, the writer Jules Sandeau revealed that he and George Sand (this was her pen name: her real name was Amantine Lucile Aurore Dudevant, née Dupin) were eating a late breakfast one morning when there was a tap on the door of the apartment. Aurore answered and the actress Marie Dorval excitedly swept into the flat, saying, 'Well, here I am.'

Each of the women recognized a kindred spirit. They became so engrossed in their conversation that Sandeau was forgotten, even though he remained close at hand for the duration of the visit. Sand and Dorval chatted for an hour, and as the latter left she invited her new friend – and Sandeau – to dine with her the following night.

Dorval's husband was on hand for the occasion, as was another guest, the poet Alfred de Vigny, who noted in his journal that George Sand elected to appear in a spectacular version of men's attire, which consisted of a close-fitting shirt, snug trousers tucked into tasselled boots and a high-crowned beaver hat. 'She looks and talks like a man,' he said, 'and has the voice and forthrightness of one. I cannot, as yet, altogether place this woman.'

In a hasty note to Sand, Marie Dorval later wrote, 'A. has made such a scene that I cannot join you as planned. But know that, until we meet, I cover you with a thousand kisses, as you shall cover me with them when I come to you.' To this George Sand replied, 'Not a thousand kisses, dear one! Ten thousand!'

26 January 1833

Do you think you will be able to bear me? You don't
yet know, and nor do I. I am so surly, so foolish, so
slow to say what is on my mind, so awkward and
tongue-tied when my heart actually has much to say!
Do not judge me on appearances. Wait a little to work
out how much mercy or affection you can afford me.

For my part, I feel that I love you with a heart
that has been made youthful and brand new again
by you. If this is a dream, as with all else I have ever
desired, do not take it from me too quickly. It does
me so much good!

Goodbye, great and beautiful one. In any case,
I shall see you this evening.

George Sand

Straightwashing 1: Frédéric Chopin (1810–1849)

In 2020 the music journalist Moritz Weber revealed in a piece written for Swiss radio entitled *Chopin's Men* that biographers had deliberately overlooked the Polish composer's relationships with men, and that his letters had been deliberately mistranslated to enhance his reputation as a ladies' man.

Chopin's ten-year relationship with George Sand has long been studied, but Weber's close inspection of Chopin's private letters revealed many declarations of love addressed to men, hints of an interest in cottaging and a description of his affairs with women as 'a cloak for hidden feelings'.

Emily Dickinson
(1830–1886)

**'We are the only poets,
and everyone else is prose.'**

The poet Emily Dickinson first met the writer Susan Huntington Gilbert (1830–1913) in 1850 at Amherst, in their native Massachusetts. Largely unknown during her lifetime, Dickinson is now acknowledged as one of the major figures of American literature, her poetry dealing with themes of death and immortality.

In various letters she described her love for Gilbert using metaphors such as the love that Dante felt for Beatrice. At least eleven of her poems were dedicated to Gilbert, but these dedications were obliterated before publication – presumably by Dickinson's acquaintance Mabel Loomis Todd, who edited the first edition of her work in 1890.

The height of their attachment, as expressed in their letters, seems to have been the summer of 1852, when Gilbert was away from Amherst. They continued to know one another throughout their lives – Gilbert married Dickinson's brother Austin in 1856 – and at Dickinson's death Gilbert dressed her in a 'simple flannel robe she had designed, laying her out in a white casket, cypripedium and violets (symbolizing faithfulness) at her neck, two heliotropes (symbolizing devotion) in her hand'.

Will you be kind to me, Susie? I am naughty and cross, this morning, and nobody loves me here; nor would you love me, if you should see me frown, and hear how loud the door bangs whenever I go through; and yet it isn't anger – I don't believe it is, for when nobody sees, I brush away big tears with the corner of my apron, and then go working on – bitter tears, Susie – so hot that they burn my cheeks, and almost scorch my eyeballs, but you have wept much, and you know they are less of anger than sorrow.

And I do love to run fast – and hide away from them all; here in dear Susie's bosom, I know is love and rest, and I never would go away, did not the big world call me, and beat me for not working … Your precious letter, Susie, it sits here now, and smiles so kindly at me, and gives me such sweet thoughts of the dear writer. When you come home, darling, I shan't have your letters, shall I, but I shall have yourself, which is more – Oh more, and better, than I can even think! I sit here with my little whip, cracking the time away, till not an hour is left of it – then you are here! And Joy is here – joy now and forevermore!

When I look around me and find myself alone, I sigh for you again; little sigh, and vain sigh, which will not bring you home.

I need you more and more, and the great world grows wider … every day you stay away – I miss my biggest heart; my own goes wandering round, and calls for Susie … Susie, forgive me Darling, for every word I say – my heart is full of you … yet when I seek to say to you something not for the world, words fail me … I shall grow more and more impatient until that dear day comes, for til now, I have only mourned for you; now I begin to hope for you.

Susan B. Anthony
(1820–1906)
&
Anna Dickinson
(1842–1932)

The social reformer and women's rights activist Susan B. Anthony played a pivotal role in the women's suffrage movement in the US. A leader of many younger activists and a national hero, she became the first female citizen to be depicted on US coinage when her portrait was used on the dollar coin in 1979.

The letters reprinted here between Anthony and the popular public speaker Anna Dickinson – her 'Dear Anna Dicky Darly' – echo the affectionate, even flirtatious, relationship Anthony had with the suffragists she mentored. With Dickinson she desires 'to snuggle … closer than ever', her bed 'big enough and good enough to take' Dickinson in. The relationship renewed her, she told Dickinson: 'Somehow your very breath gives me new hope and new life.' In turn, Dickinson reveals to Anthony a longing 'to hold your hand in mine, to hear your voice, in a word, I want you'.

Auburn Dec. 6 1866

My Dearest Anna

I am so glad you are at your own dear home with
your mother and sister – I got Susie's note from
Rockford – but the telegraph wires had lightened
my anxiety before – and yesterday's Tribune scares
me again – by its item that you are going to speak
so soon – I beg you be "patient waiter" for such you
know is given the crown at last –

And, darling, you must not die until you have
rounded out your glorious testimonies to the full
orbit of human attainment – and to make sure, you
must go slow now –

But – Anna – I am going to Philadelphia the 15th
inst[ead] – Wednesday [week] and hope to snuggle
you darling closer than ever – If prayers will avail
& prevail to hold you in the body, and save you to
God's highest, Grandest work here – you'll not go
or fail –

Shall I come to you – your precious Mother and
sister gave me so cordial a greeting & so hearty an
invitation to do so I don't know but I should go if
you say so. I go into Rochester Tuesday – I am at

The Love That Dares

Ms. Wright's – sister of Lucretia Mitts – We have [a] meeting here tomorrow – Ms. Pillsbury and Miss Disher to come – they at Clifton Springs today –

Miss B. is very promising – but of course I cannot feel sure yet – if she only has the solid granite at bottom which she now seems to have – she will grow & take high place – I can't tell you what joy it is to even find a hope –

Anna – at this distance I mark you for our Spring Anniversary – our first Equal Rights Anniversary – It will be Thursday May 9th –

I enclose a [trust] we have – Are you vexed with me? – but every body says your word is the prettiest little gem possible specially the hundred dollars –

It is perfectly wonderful – the change of tone of Pulpit & Press toward us – do you see the Ohio legislature starts off with [a] proposition to amend State Con. for all women & colored people to vote – the Universal Suffrage ship is [fairly] set each –

Lovingly yours – S.B.A.

11 November 1869

Dearly Loved Anna

How I have missed you & yet how I have longed to
meet you – for more reasons than one – I shall try
& meet you at Albany – the 16th – or at Rondout
– unless you are coming here right after – I must see
you & can't put it on paper –
                    My heart is full
                    Affectionately
                    S.B. Anthony

To Susan B. Anthony

If ever for thy love I had a penchant
I fear thy heart would not esteem it valid
For thou hast said: 'I'm positive that men shan't
Ever to wedlock lead me.' Thou hast rallied
The female sex, from Boston to Sumatra
Strong-minded ones, of mind and manner various,
But each is firm; though all men coax and flatter her
They build their hopes in bases most precarious

Oscar Wilde
(1854–1900)
&
Walt Whitman
(1819–1892)

In 1882, as part of his year-long lecture tour of North America – a sojourn which took him among silver miners in Colorado as well as the elite of New York and Boston – the twenty-seven-year-old Oscar Wilde made a pilgrimage of sorts to Camden, New Jersey, to visit the poet Walt Whitman, whose collection *Leaves of Grass* (1855) made no attempt to conceal his love for men.

The first of the two letters that follow is from Wilde to Whitman, full of the gushing praise and excitement of a young man who has found acceptance from an older mentor he admires and seeks to emulate. The second letter is from Whitman to his lover Harry Stafford (1858–1918) and in part describes Wilde's visit.

[March 1882]
1267 Broadway, New York

My Dear Dear Walt –

Swinburne[1] has just written to me to say as follows.

'I am sincerely interested and gratified by your account of Walt Whitman and the assurance of his kindly and friendly feeling towards me: and I thank you, no less sincerely, for your kindness in sending me word of it. As sincerely can I say, what I shall be freshly obliged to you if you will assure him of in my name, that I have by no manner of means relaxed my admiration of his noblest works – such parts, above all, of his writings, as treat of the noblest subjects, material and spiritual, with which poetry can deal – I have always thought it, and I believe it will be hereafter generally thought his highest and surely most enviable distinction that he never speaks so well as when he speaks of great matters – Liberty, for instance, and Death.

1   'Swinburne' is the English poet Algernon Charles Swinburne (1837–1909).

'This of course does not imply that I do, or rather it implies that I do not agree with all his theories, or admire all his work in anything like equal measure

– a form of admiration which I should by no means desire for myself and am as little prepared to bestow on another – considering it a form of scarcely indirect insult.'

There! You see how you remain in our hearts – and how simply and grandly Swinburne speaks of you knowing you to be simple and grand yourself.

Will you in return send me for Swinburne a copy of your Essay on Poetry – the pamphlet – with your name and his on it – it would please him so much. Before I leave America I must see you again – there is no one in this wide great world of America whom I love and honor so much.

With warm affection, and honorable admiration,
Oscar Wilde

... from Walt Whitman
to Harry Stafford

[January 1882]

Dear Harry

Yours rec'd – I am just starting off a few miles out
from Phila[dephia] – probably a day or two only –
will look up the book you require (if I can find one)
soon as I come back – & send you – I am ab't as
usual – nothing very new –

– Hank if I'd known you was coming home last
Sunday would have come down Saturday & staid till
Monday any way – You say you wrote a blue letter
but didn't send it to me – dear boy the only way is
to dash ahead and 'whistle dull cares away' – after
all it's mostly in one's self one gets blue & not from
outside – life is like the weather – you've got to take
what comes, & you can make it all go pretty well if
only think so (& provide in reason for rain & snow) –

– I wish it was so you could all your life come in
& see me often for an hour or two – You see I think
I understand you better than any one – (& like you
more too) – (You may not fancy so, but it is so) – &

I believe Hank there are many things, confidences, questions, candid says you would like to have with me, you have never yet broached – me the same –

 – Have you read about Oscar Wilde? – He has been to see me & spent an afternoon – He is a fine large handsome youngster – had the good sense to take a great fancy to me! – I was invited to receptions in Phila. am[on]g the big bugs & a grand dinner to him by Mr & Mrs Childs – but did not go to any – Awful cold here, this is now the third day, – but you know all about that – (you say you know you are a great fool – don't you know every 'cute fellow secretly knows that about himself – I do) – God bless you my darling boy – Keep a brave heart –

W W

Straightwashing 2: Oscar Wilde

Many biographies of Wilde have been written since his death in 1900, but it wasn't until 2018 that one combined openness about his sexuality with a scholarly approach considered rigorous enough by the academics. *Oscar: A Life* by Matthew Sturgis was hailed as the first truly comprehensive account of Wilde's life – emotional and sexual as well as literary.

The earlier biographies were not the only instances of ignominy continuing even after death. Jacob Epstein's sculpture of a sphinx that marks Wilde's grave at Père Lachaise Cemetery in Paris, which was unveiled in 1914, was immediately defaced when the figure's proud member and exposed testicles were covered over in plaster. In 1961 the sculpture was attacked again. A replacement silver prosthesis created by multimedia artist Leon Johnson was installed in 2000.

Dame Ethel Mary Smyth
(1858–1944)

Dame Ethel Smyth was a British composer, suffragette and memoirist. She never married and had no children. She came of age in Victorian England, when wife and mother were the only 'acceptable' roles for women – which did not appeal to her nature in the slightest. She travelled extensively throughout Europe, where she studied, played and composed music. In 1910 she joined the Women's Social and Political Union (not least because of her crush on Emmeline Pankhurst) and was so committed to the suffrage movement she ended up in Holloway Prison for two months for 'window smashing'. It was there that she famously led her fellow prisoners in a rendition of her suffragette anthem 'The March of Women', conducting with her toothbrush.

Despite making no secret of her love for women, Smyth still struggled to accept her sexuality, as she describes in a letter to her dear friend Henry Brewster (1850–1908).

A year later she wrote to Brewster about Lady Mary Ponsonby (1832–1916), with whom she had, she said, 'one of the longest, closest, most joy-giving relations of my life'. Mary Ponsonby, the granddaughter of former prime minister Charles Grey, the 2nd Earl Grey, was a lady-in-waiting to Queen Victoria.

Smyth also formed a lifelong relationship with Mary Benson (1841–1918), widow of Edward White Benson (1829–96), the archbishop of Canterbury. Smyth once said of Benson that she was 'as good as God, and as clever as the Devil', which 'struck such resonance among those who knew [Benson] well, that it did the rounds of their friends'. Her letter to Benson here also makes clear the strength of Smyth's feelings. Benson herself was bisexual, and Smyth found in her a fondness and camaraderie with another woman who failed to fit the Victorian template of womanhood. After her husband died, Benson shared a house and a life with Lucy Tait (1856–1938), daughter of the previous archbishop of Canterbury, Arthur Campbell Tait (1811–82).

... to Henry Brewster

October 6, 1892

... I suppose you know [August Graf von] Platen's poems? I've just been reading Heine's 'Reisebilder'. Surely anything funnier was never written. And as for his remarks on Platen's admiration for Greek homosexuality, and his contention that the whole beauty of Shakespeare's Sonnets derives from their being written or at least most of them to a boy ... well, you can imagine Heine on this theme!

I wonder why it is so much easier for me, and I believe for a great many English women, to love my own sex passionately rather than yours? Even my love for my mother had an intense quality you can only call passion. How do you account for it? I can't make it out for I think I am a very healthy-minded person and it is an everlasting puzzle ...

Selaby. February 27, 1893

... I don't blame you for calling the arrival of Lady Ponsonby on the scene 'One of your grand discoveries of the right person.' But Harry you know one must search, and mistake, and find 'better', and 'better still' till 'the best' is found. And this is the best. I told her, and I tell you, I am like the old lady who said to the burglar under her bed, 'I've been looking for you all my life and at last I've found you!'

She's difficult to describe; moody, sensitive, and (one feels it) as fatally steadfast as I am myself. Only in her case sceptical philosophy runs through everything and makes her doubt the evidence of her own senses; she reads everything and believes in nothing save the ideal. A mixture of passionate impulse and passionate reticence; ascetic, and a sybarite; courageous, direct, and on occasion as veiled as Isis. I should judge that in most respects her sensuous life is as strong as that of most women in their prime; as my own for instance; and added to all a dignity that would never leave her in the lurch a taste that is infallible.

There now! can you at all guess the fascination and impressiveness of the whole 'Erscheinung' [appearance] and understand what it is to me to have made her fond of me? ... and I mustn't forget what I care for most in a way ... her relation to her family ... the hold she has, as companion in daily life, in trouble, laughter, problems of statesmanship on her husband ... and as supreme influence on her children.

The Love That Dares

... to Lady Ponsonby

Frimhurst. September 14, 1893

About your speaking voice, it is profoundly true
that voices mean more to me than anything
almost, and your voice is ... you. Well, sometimes
when we are apart, I try to hear it and can't.
Anyone else's, yes, but not yours. I remember that
in illicit Encyclopaedia readings in bygone years
(I would resume them, only alas! there are so few
things I don't know about nowadays!) there was
a long jaw about impotence resulting from over-
desire. 'I'm all right with other women' the patient
would say to the doctor, 'but that one unmans
me.' How I used to ponder over that sentence,
and dimly sympathise with the unfortunate man!
I suppose it's that sort of thing about your voice;
I long too violently to hear it.

... to Mary Benson

I see you as I have always seen you, and love you
as I have always loved you. True, the thing has not
grown into what I expected; as a rule if you love
much and imagine you are loved, much intercourse
ensues, but in our case this could not be, and very
naturally we feel a certain sadness about it. But let
me, just for once, say this. The reasons for which
I love you are unshakable; here are some of them;
your truth, your fire, your intensity, your power of
sustained effort, your extraordinary grip over other
souls, your intellect, and above all, in the words of
a prayer I like, your 'unconquerable heart.' And
playing on it all is the recollection of that firm hand
in mine ...

Hidden Notes of Love

There are hundreds of examples of composers penning musical love letters to their dearest ones. Queer composers were no exception, of course, but in the face of prejudice and anti-gay legislation, often these messages of love had to be coded in some way as well.

In a piece written for Pride month 2019, on the New York classical music radio station WQXR's blog, soprano Heather O'Donovan compiled a list of musical dedications by LGBTQ+ composers. These included pieces such as Pyotr Tchaikovsky's 'My Genius, My Angel, My Friend' (1857), dedicated to Sergey Kireyev; Ethel Smyth's 'The March of the Women' (1911), written for Emmeline Pankhurst, leader of the suffragist movement; the collaboration between Gian Carlo Menotti and Samuel Barber on the opera *Vanessa* (1956); and Lou Harrison's 'Music for Bill and Me' (1967), Bill being Bill Colvig, whom Harrison had just met and who was his partner for the next thirty-three years. Another composer highlighted was Francis Poulenc, who in a letter that accompanied his *Concert champêtre* wrote to his lover Richard

Chanlaire: 'I offer [this] ... to you today because you are the being that I cherish most upon this earth. You have changed my life, you are ... my reason for living and for working.'

As O'Donovan writes, 'Today, these musical love letters can be viewed ... as small acts of subversion' – and we can honour them now as a means by which LGBTQ+ composers could express and celebrate their love and lovers without risk of persecution.

Katharine Lee Bates
(1859–1929)

Katharine Lee Bates was an American professor of English literature at Wellesley College, Massachusetts, best known for writing the lyrics to 'America the Beautiful'. For twenty-five years she lived with Katharine Coman (1857–1915), an economic historian, social activist and colleague at Wellesley.

While some historians have classified Bates and Coman's relationship as a 'Boston marriage' – after Henry James's 1886 novel *The Bostonians*, which featured two unmarried women who lived together – they were examples of the late 19th-century feminist ideal of 'New Women', defined by historian Ruth Bordin as 'women who exercised control over their own lives be it personal, social, or economic'.

American historian Lilian Faderman has found that the term 'Wellesley marriage' became interchangeable with 'Boston marriage' because of how popular Bates and Coman were at the college.

For women like Bates and Coman, marriage would have been the end of their working careers and the beginning of child-rearing and domesticity.

Historian Judith Schwarz thinks that it is 'obvious' from the book of poetry that Bates wrote after Coman's death that she felt a 'yearning desire that glows throughout the poems ... that the two women were more than just friends ... [they] were a devoted lesbian couple'.

Bates and Coman destroyed almost all of their decades-long correspondence. Nevertheless we can appreciate the power of Bates's beautiful words in the handful of letters that remain.

You are having your way at last and I'm bravely beginning on the letter-a-fortnight plan, but I don't like it. It makes me so lonesome … You mustn't write me oftener than once a fortnight. That will only be putting temptation in my way, for I always want to answer a letter of yours the hour it comes.

… I wonder if an English spring can be as beautiful as Princeton was a year ago. Do you remember the sunset sky that Sunday evening, when we strayed home from the Rock and there were two hands in one pocket? We'll go to Princeton again sometime.

For I am coming back to you, my Dearest, whether I come back to Wellesley or not. You are always in my heart and in my longing. I've been so homesick for you on this side of the ocean and yet so still and happy in the memory and consciousness of you. It was the living away from you that made, at first, the prospect of leaving Wellesley so heartachy … It was never very possible to leave Wellesley [for good], because so many love-anchors held me there, and it seemed least of all possible when I had just found the long-desired way to your dearest heart

… Of course I want to come to you, very much as I want to come to Heaven … The winter, since you and I can't tell each other anything but the truth, has been rather retrograde … I'm going to Oxford to rest and watch the Spring. I shall live very quietly and do my faithful best to get well. But I'm tired of taking care of your Katharine. If I bring her back to you, will you take care of her yourself? Sweetheart, I always love you, more dearly than you know. Please take care of my Katharine.

Edward Carpenter
(1844–1929)
&
George Merrill
(1867–1928)

For over twenty years the socialist, vegetarian, writer and campaigner Edward Carpenter lived openly with his lover, George Merrill – who had been a labourer in a Sheffield ironworks – at their home in Millthorpe, outside Sheffield. A great influence on later generations, Carpenter befriended, among others, E.M. Forster, who visited 'Ted' and George and tried to follow their happy example by more openly sharing his life with his married lover, the policeman Robert Buckingham.

Sheffield City Archives hold much of Edward Carpenter's correspondence and writings, including an affectionate biography, 'George Merrill. A true history, & study in Psychology' (1913), extracts from which follow.

[5 March 1913]

I have known George Merrill now for some twenty-two years … It is not often perhaps that two people are associated over a longish period so closely as we have been; for though the ordinary man and wife may see a good deal of each other, yet it generally happens in that case that their respective occupations carry them during the day pretty far apart; whereas in our case we have been practically within hail of one another all the time – working side by side in the garden or that house, or at most in adjacent rooms, meeting at nearly every meal, plunging together over the hills to the railway station and into Sheffield, or travelling in England or abroad. And I think it speaks well for both of us that the relation has endured this somewhat severe test: – that it has grown indeed in grace; and that our intimacy, though perhaps a little different in its temperamental character, is just as close and sincere to-day as it was twenty years ago.

Later in the manuscript Carpenter describes George's 'very sweet [singing] voice', saying:

The Love That Dares

This gift of song was very much the key to George's character, which had all the fine spontaneity and subtlety of the musical temperament. He found his way to people's hearts as simply and surely as a thrush or a blackbird. And his occasionally Elizabethan language and jokes, caught originally from the alleys in which he was born were (though a little shocking to some people) really too humorous and human to be out of keeping with his native refinement.

Carpenter also recounts how they met, 'some time early in 1891':

It was in a railway carriage, coming from Sheffield to Totley ... We exchanged a few words and a look of recognition; but it was no time for talk, for on leaving the train at Totley quite a little party joined me ... and I was compelled to walk with them. However I soon found that at a little distance behind George was following us ... His appealing look even at that distance reached me.

And of when they first moved in together:

> I received no end of letters, kindly meant, but full
> of warnings and advice – deprecating the idea of a
> menage without a woman, as a thing unheard of,
> and a step entered on, it was supposed, in a rash
> moment, without due consideration; hinting at the
> risk to my health, to my comfort, at bad cooking,
> untidy rooms, and abundance of cobwebs, not to
> mention the queer look of the thing, the remarks
> of neighbours, the certainty that the arrangement
> could not last long, and so forth.

The letters here are just two from many Merrill sent to
Carpenter expressing his affection and devotion. The
spelling has been kept as in the originals.

Millthorpe

Friday

Don't be cross with me *dear dad* don't think because
I have not written to you I have not thought about
you, for I have, every hour of the day. I have had
nothing of any importance to write about excepting
we three have been very happy and all kept wishing
you was with us we shall all be so glad to see *thee*
back again especially your humble servant. And dear
one I have not been idle whilst thou as been away
but when near post time I have felt to lazy to write.
how much I have missed thee dear no one but myself
knows I have been very good and only been out
once by myself that was last night and Kate was to
tired to go with me I'm busy to day cleaning up stairs
and bakeing and Max and Kate are sitting outside it
is very warm here to day but not much sun. I should
like to come down to Sheffield so I think I will but
don't know what time but sure to be in at Glover
Rd and I will come there before six. I am arrangeing
to see my Mother some where near the Station to
have a chat with her as I shall not be going down to
Sheffield for a few more weeks. Jack and Max both

send there love and are looking forward to seeing thee back. I hope you will see G. H to night before he goes away Kate and I was at there house on Wenesday night fond love from thy own Geo x

Wenesday

My Dearest Ted, so please to hear from you, but am so dreadfully busy papering, no time to write much. It looks very nice what we have done. I had a letter from Frank D. who is going to write you. I hope you had a nice time crossing for we had a fearful snowstorm here yesterday, and went pitch dark Max is keeping well and sends love write soon dear. I felt rather anxious about you yesterday dear when I thought you was on the water much love to Arnold and much more to thy self

thine always Geo

Siegfried Sassoon
(1886–1967)

The poet, soldier and writer Siegfried Sassoon is perhaps best known for his anti-war poetry, born out of his experiences in the First World War and his anger at the waste and devastation he saw there. Born into a family of cultured and talented Iraqi Jews (on his father's side) and Anglo-Catholics (on his mother's), Sassoon was educated at Marlborough and Cambridge before embarking on a career as a writer, his first published success being *The Daffodil Murderer* in 1913. Sassoon sent the letter that follows three years before the war, and after reading Edward Carpenter's book *The Intermediate Sex* (1908) to express his gratitude for the affirmation and acceptance he found there for his own deepest feelings and desires.

Weirleigh, Paddock Wood, Kent
July 27th, 1911

Dear Edward Carpenter

I am sending you a few sonnets; not for what is
in them, but to thank you for all that I reverence
and am grateful for in you & your writings. It was
not until October last year, when I was just 24,
that, by accident, I read your 'Intermediate Sex',
& have since read 'Towards Democracy' & 'Who
shall command the heart'. I am afraid I have not
studied socialism sufficiently to be in sympathy with
what I know of it; but your words have shown me
all that I was blind to before, & have opened up
the new life for me, after a time of great perplexity
& unhappiness. Until I read 'The Intermediate
Sex', I knew absolutely nothing of that subject,
(& was entirely unspolted, as I am now), but life
was an empty thing, & what ideas I had about
homosexuality were absolutely prejudiced, & I
was in such a groove that I couldn't allow myself
to be what I wished to be, & the intense attraction
I felt for my own sex was almost a subconscious
thing, & my antipathy for women a mystery to

me. It was only by chance that (when I had read yr book) I found my brother (a year younger) was exactly the same. I cannot say what it has done for me. I am a different being, & have a definite aim in life & something to lean on, though, of course the misunderstanding & injustice is a bitter agony sometimes. But having found out all about it, I am old enough to realise the better & nobler way, & to avoid the mire which might have snared me, had I known 5 years ago. I write to you as the leader & the prophet.

I am afraid my life is occupied a good deal with things that you may not approve. I live here mostly, in the country with my mother, cricket in summer, & riding & hunting in winter; & I am thankful to say I am as good as those others in their sports, & have some of their strength & courage. My other life is all taken up with poetry & an intense passion for music, (though I am *not a brilliant* player). Anyhow I am not mixed up with smartness & luxurious social doings, as my name might lead you to think. I am a nephew of Hamo Thornycroft, the sculptor. I send a photograph, as I know you are interested in our cases; which is the reason why I have written you so much in the egotistic strain. The only other book

I have read is Symond's 'Problem in Greek Ethics'.
My father died in 1894 aged 35. He was a nephew of
Sir Albert Sassoon & those other plutocrats; he was
intensely musical, & I think had a strong vein of the
homosexual nature in him.

I hope you are well and I am sure you are happy
& at peace with this bitter world. May your reward
be in the generations to come, as I pray mine may
be. I am not religious, but I try to believe that our
immortality is to be, (in those immortals whom our
better lives may lead to, & whose immortal ways
are marred & kept back by the grossness of our
unworthy souls.) I take as my watchword those
words of yours, – strength to perform, & pride to
suffer without sign

from
Siegfried Sassoon

[p.s.] The most recent photo was taken at Oxford,
by Nevill Fortas, who has spoken to me about you a
great deal.

Vita Sackville-West
(1892–1962)

Vita Sackville-West was a bisexual writer, perhaps best known today for her affairs with various women (including Virginia Woolf) while remaining married to her husband, Harold Nicolson, who was also bisexual. But before Harold entered Vita's life, her heart had been claimed by another. Vita and Violet Keppel Trefusis met as children and their relationship became romantic as teenagers. At the age of fourteen Violet even gave Vita a ring symbolizing their love.

However, Vita's appetite for life and for love was more suited for polyamory. Violet's mother compounded the couple's difficulties. Desperate to break them up, she arranged for Violet to marry Denys Trefusis. Violet agreed on the condition that he never ask her for sex, though it's said that she also agreed as a means of getting back at Vita, who had herself become engaged to marry Harold. Despite being separated, Vita and Violet stayed in each other's lives for the rest of their lives, often through letters.

We simply could not have this nice, simple, naif, childish connexion without its turning into a passionate love-affair again.

If you have any honesty in your nature, you will agree with me.

You and I cannot be together. I go down country lanes and meet a notice saying 'Beware. Unexploded bomb'.

So I have to go around another way.

You are the unexploded bomb to me.

I don't want you to explode.

I don't want you to disrupt my life.

My quiet life is dear to me. I hate being dragged away from it. Like Dorothy, I have become *maniaque*.

Just as Dorothy gets the doors left open for fear of germs, so do I stick at home among my cabbages.

This letter will anger you. I do not care if it does, since I know that no anger or irritation will ever destroy the love that exists between us.

And if you really want me, I will come to you, always, anywhere.

You see, you said we might have two sorts of capital to draw on: the great tragedy sort and the childhood-friendship sort. That is true in a way – but not wholly true. You know quite well, if you face it honestly, that although the childhood-friendship link between us is strong and important, the other sort matters equally.

Mitya

LETTER NO. 57 (extract)
Sissinghurst Castle January 27, 1941

Lushka,

I write to you in a bad temper with nearly all my world, always excepting Harold who is a permanent delight – but whom I see only at weekends. He is so refreshing, so unpetty, so amusing, so much the best of the French and English temperaments combined. You would like him now that you have no personal cause to dislike him.

As I said, I write in a bad temper. My world, my life, is getting complicated at this moment and I hate that. I really hate that.

And that is one of the reasons I don't want to get involved with you again: I really dislike the complications and intrigues that your life entails. They bore me.

I love you, and shall always love you, but I would never be bothered with all your maze and labyrinth of life. I don't want to fall in love with you all over again.

I've said this before: so "*glissons, mortels, n'y attardons nous pas.*" (I've quoted incorrectly, I know. You know the quotation I mean. It was a favourite of yours, once.)

Natalie Clifford Barney
(1876–1972)

Born in Dayton Ohio, the playwright and poet Natalie Clifford Barney first knew love with Eva Palmer (1874–1952), whom she had met on a beach in Bar Harbor, Maine, in 1893. Referring to Palmer as the 'mother of my desires', Barney found in her a kindred spirit who shared her love for Sappho and 'dreamed of a utopia, modelled on Sappho's community on the island of Lesbos, where creative women supported and loved each other'.

Barney moved to France in 1899, where she truly blossomed. An heiress, her home at 20 rue Jacob in Paris became a literary salon for more than sixty years. Every Friday between 4 and 8 p.m. people arrived to share in, as Diana Souhami describes, 'the cutting edge of art, the conversation, the strawberry tarts and the prospect of finding lovers and friends'. Here Barney had a sign crafted and hung in her garden which echoed Sappho's words: *À L'AMITIÉ* – *To Friendship*. To gals being pals.

It was at her salon that Barney met one of her lovers, Dolly Wilde (1895–1941). Born Dorothy Ierne Wilde in the year her uncle Oscar was imprisoned, Dolly grew up in his shadow and even looked like him – 'except that she was handsome', as the American journalist Janet Flanner (1892–1978) quipped. During the First World War, Wilde travelled to Paris to drive ambulances as part of the war effort. There she met Marion 'Joe' Carstairs (1900–93) with whom she had an affair. Carstairs went on to have affairs with Greta Garbo, Marlene Dietrich and Tallulah Bankhead, but she and Wilde remained friends after ending their romantic relationship.

Wilde was indeed wild about Barney, but though she was Wilde's longest relationship, Natalie was a devout and unapologetic polyamorist. She described herself as 'fidèle infidèle', by which she meant she would remain faithful to her lovers in all ways save sex. Her romance with Wilde flickered on and off for fourteen years, until Dolly's tragically early death. Wilde struggled with her addictions to alcohol and heroin, and in 1939 she was diagnosed with breast cancer. She refused traditional treatment and died the following year at age 45, either from cancer or a drug overdose.

... from Dolly Wilde

I have put a match to a perfectly laid fire & sit contentedly in this mysterious world of fire-light & lamp-light at a strange, enchanted hour. Free from pain I have stretched luxuriously & savoured quiet thoughts in my charming room. You walk down the avenues of mind, peacefully, wonderfully ...

Do you love me? I wonder. Not that it matters at all. Perhaps I shan't even mind when you leave me – only then there could be no love-making – impossible thought ... I give you eternity as a (terrifying!) guarantee ... of my love, while you beg for favours because the end is so near! Who will flee first? Just now I am too in love with you to dream of change, & grant you precedence darling ...

Did you know that it was nearly four o'clock when I left you last night? I ache with tiredness and darling I am bruised.

Toujours, D.

[20 July 1927]

Oh! Darling I am fallen from grace, sadly! Last night a starry night outside my windows and the exciting darkness full of your presence. I was assailed by the most furious desires ... No listless surrender this to your memory, Natalie – but irresistible, tremulous ecstatic passion lifting one high on the crest of imagination of love, leaving one finally shaken and exhausted with one's heart furiously beating against one's side ... and with all my knowledge I possessed you as deeply and as actually as if you had been there ... that blinding lightning – like possession too swift, too acutely felt ... I sought quick comfort in excess [and] it was you who soothed me with your own desire this time and filled me with that well-remembered delight. Oh! The force of your love as you gave it; making me cry out; darling ...

Never Being Boring

The lyrics to the Pet Shop Boys' elegy to friends lost to AIDS, 'Being Boring', mention the spouse of a 1920s writer. The writer in question (the clues are there!) was F Scott Fitzgerald, whose novels include *The Great Gatsby* and *Tender Is the Night*, and who with his wife Zelda formed the heart of an enclave of queer and straight writers and artists in Paris in the mid-1920s. The quote comes from Zelda's response to news of the death of a friend: 'She was never bored because she was never boring.'

Eleanor Roosevelt

The diplomat and activist Eleanor Roosevelt was First Lady (wife of President Franklin Delano Roosevelt) from 1933 to 1944. A stalwart social campaigner throughout the world, she served as US Delegate to the United Nations General Assembly (1945–52) and championed the creation of the Freedom from Hunger campaign. Eleanor met the journalist Lorena Hickok (1893–1968) in 1928, when Hickok was assigned to interview her for the Associated Press. Hickok covered Roosevelt during FDR's 1932 presidential election campaign, and a friendship began that would last over thirty years. Roosevelt was soon writing to Hickok daily, in missives that were ten or fifteen pages long each. The nature of their relationship has been subject to debate among historians, and as is often the case we are left to judge the evidence of the letters for ourselves. What cannot be questioned by anyone who takes the time to learn more about these two women is the impact of their close relationship on their lives. Their letters and relationship are the subject of several excellent books, including *Empty Without You* by Rodger Streitmatter and *Eleanor and Hick* by Susan Quinn.

Radclyffe/John Hall
(1880–1943)

Radclyffe Hall is perhaps best known for her novel *The Well of Loneliness*, which made headline news in 1928 for portraying the story of a gender-noncomforming woman named Stephen who, like Hall, described herself as an 'invert', the word at the time for a woman who loved other women. Hall went by the name 'Radclyffe' professionally, but personally she went by and signed her letters 'John'.

An heiress, Hall was at liberty to live and love as she chose. At the age of twenty-seven and in classic lesbian fashion, she fell in love with an older woman, Mabel Batten (1856–1916), who was then fifty-one. Batten was the first to call her 'John', and they set up house together for the next eight years, until Hall fell in love with Batten's cousin Una Troubridge (1887–1963). Mabel Batten was absolutely devastated and died less than a year later.

Hall and Troubridge remained together until Hall's death. However, they became involved in another love triangle. On holiday in the mid-1930s, Hall fell ill and went to hospital, where she met and fell in love with her nurse, Evguenia Souline. Troubridge hated the fact that Hall couldn't end her relationship with Souline but she never left Hall.

As the long letters to Souline below show, Hall had little interest in spelling and was no fan of the apostrophe. After some debate, we have decided not to interfere with her style.

A small note on pronouns. As evidenced in the letter that follows, Hall used the term 'invert' to describe herself. The term comes from the Havelock Ellis' titular work 'Sexual Inversion', the first English medical textbook on homosexuality, where he defines an 'invert' as 'sexual instinct turned by inborn constitutional abnormality toward persons of the same sex'. In another letter to Souline, Hall writes at length defending Souline's attraction to Hall as natural because same-sex attraction is natural. Hall also writes, 'For me to sleep with a man would be "wrong" because it would be an outrage against nature.' Though Hall used the name John, it is for these reasons that we used 'she/her' for Hall.

[Sirmione]
Tuesday July 31st 1934

My beloved. I do not know how I have the strength
to write what must be written – it is this: I cannot see
you in Paris on my way back to England. I had been
counting on this – I had thought I shall see her once
more before I go back and take up the burden of my
everyday life – perhaps I shall see her several times
even; it was something that Una said that made
me dare to hope. And then in Paris she seemed so
merciful. You remember that she sent you her love
and said that she would write to you, then yesterday
she did actually write to you. Last evening I got your
letter in answer to mine written on Friday before I
left for Italy, and your letter made me long so much
to see you and touch you and hear you speak if only
once again, and I said: 'I shall try to see Soulina on
my way home, I shall go and see her.' And somehow,
God know why, I thought Una would consent, for
she knows how it is with me, with us, and she knows
too something that I have not told you: she knows
that I am ill with misery – not seriously ill, nothing
for you to worry about, but all is not very well with
me, which in the circumstances is natural. Then I

found that she means to keep us apart. I dare not blame her, I do not blame her. She and I have been together for 17 years. When all the world seemed to be against me at the time of the 'Well of Loneliness' persecution, Una stood shoulder to shoulder with me, fighting every inch of that terrific battle. She has given me all of her interest and indeed of her life ever since we made common cause, therefore she has the right to do what she is doing and she will not cede that right, but insists on it with all the strength which lies – as she well knows – in her physical weakness. It has been very terrible, she has reminded me of her operation, of every illness she had through the years. She has told me that she is very ill now, that [her doctor] warned her to avoid all emotion, that if I do see you everything will happen between us, and that then she could never be happy again but would fret herself until she died. She says that she will not tolerate our meeting. When I said that I would control myself if only I could see you again, she would not believe me, and this morning, after a scene which lasted all night, she suddenly hurled herself onto the floor and looked as though she were going demented. I think that it may very well be that her operation has made her more excitable – women are like that after that operation. Then she has reminded me over & over again until I have nearly gone mad, that I have always stood for fidelity in the case of inverted unions, that the eyes of the inverted all over the world are turned towards me, that they look up to me, in a word, that for years now they have respected me because my own union has been faithful and open. And when she says this I can find no answer, because she is only telling the truth – I have tried to help my poor kind by setting an example, especially of courage, and thousands have turned to me for help and found it, if I may believe their letters, and she says that I want to betray my inverts who look upon me almost as their leader. Oh, but whats the use of telling you any more of the hell that I went through last night & this morning – I have a debt of honour to pay, i am under terrific obligation, and can I shirk the intolerable load? It is less whether I can shirk my load than whether I have the strength to bear it. But one small comfort would Una concede, she agrees that we shall write to each other – I think she knows that there comes a stage when human nature can no longer endure, and that I simply cannot endure never hearing from you – that would kill me, I should die, Soulina. The

thought, the knowledge, that you are in the world,
& might be suffering, in trouble, in poverty, even
ill perhaps and so terribly alone, having neither
parents nor country, and you so small somehow –
well, I just could not bear it. As it is I remember that
you were once ill, seriously ill and so little money
– and sometimes I cannot sleep at night because
you do not take care of yourself, and because I
cannot take care of you. And I think of a thousand
worrying things, I think: 'Has she got two pairs of
glasses – does she keep an extra pair in her bag in
case she breaks her frames in the street – if she does
not do this, keep an extra pair, she is so very blind
that one day she may get run over.' Then I think: 'Is
she careful not to catch cold – will she be careful this
coming winter? Does she get terribly over tired? Does
she eat enough good & nourishing food?' These
are the kidneys of thoughts that will come when I
lie awake thinking about you. Therefore if you love
me as I love you you will write to me, Soulina. You
will let me know any change of address, you will let
me know what you are doing – you will let me know
whether you are well or ill – prosperous or in need of
help – and this you will do out of your compassion.
And I will write to you also. And if you refuse to

write, Soulina – then God help me, I don't think
that I can go on, for I am almost too desolate as it
is, to go on living. Its so strange and rather terrible
to be as I have been since I met you – I feel that I
am no longer myself – I am nothing at all but one
great ache – I think I have told you think already.
And I cannot remember that I have a career, that I
am quite a well know[n] writer – that all seems like a
dream – and as vague as a dream; and I cannot seem
to associate myself with my friends and my home in
England anymore. Like you, I am homeless & I have
no country. In your letter of the 28th you ask me if
love can be only spiritual – why surely there can be
a love of the spirit, and this love I think I must have
for you as well as a love of the body. But oh, my
God, I am so terribly unhappy – haunted too by an
unendurable fear that I have made you unhappy. I
who would lay down my life for you have only made
you suffer through me. Why did we have to meet, we
two? What do we mean you & I to each other? And
listen, my beloved, what have we done that you &
I must punish each other? I don't think that I shall
ever write another book – I think that something in
me has gone out – I think that in parting with you I
am finished.

And now I am going to ask a great favour which of your charity you will grant me. I know that just now you are hard pressed for money, you must be in present conditions in France, &n if you write & tell me that this is not so I shall simply not believe you, Soulina. I want to send you £100. I want you to spend a little on me in stamps for those letters that you will write me – for the rest I want you to buy yourself small comforts. It is not for the others ... it is only for the one that I love, I insist that you spend it all on yourself – that is what I want you to do to please me. But put a few pounds aside, if you will, just in case you wanted to send me a cable – you might want more help – one never knows, and perhaps you might even want my help quickly ... And this is the only drop of comfort I have, that I can send you a small sum of money ... For some reason, Una wants to stay on, but I do not – it is too beautiful – I cannot endure its beauty just now – always my heart cries out for you to share it. I think I had better go back to England, but Una does not feel well enough, she says, and if this is so I must not force her. God bless you and keep you heart of my heart – my joy & my unbelievable grief, for that is what you have become to me, Soulina.

John

24 October 1934

Why is it that the people I write of are so very often
lonely people? Are they? I think that perhaps you
may be right. I greatly feel the loneliness of the soul –
nearly every soul is more or less lonely. Then again:
I have been called the writer of 'misfits.' And it
may be that being myself a 'misfit,' for as you know,
beloved, I am a born invert, it may be that I am a
writer of 'misfits' in one form or another – I think
I understand them – their joys & their sorrows,
indeed I know I do, and all the misfits of this world
are lonely, being conscious that they differ from the
rank and file. When we meet you & I will talk of my
work and you shall be my critic, my darling. If you
wish to you shall be very rude – but I do hope you
like your John's work just a little. I want you to like
my work, Soulina.

Darling – I wonder if you realize how much I am
counting on your coming to England, how much it
means to me – it means all the world, and indeed
my body shall be all, all yours, as yours will be all,
all mine, beloved. And we two will lie close in each
other's arms, close, close, always trying to lie even
closer, and I will kiss your mouth and your eyes and

your breasts – I will kiss your body all over – And you shall kiss me back again many times as you kissed me when we were in Paris. And nothing will matter but just we two, we two longing loves at last come together. I wake up in the night & think of these things & then I can't sleep for my longing, Soulina. This is love – make no mistake about it – love has come to you – you are loved and loved. No one whom you meet is more loved than you are – no one in the whole world can be more loved. When you look at people you can say to yourself in your heart – 'I also has got a lover – I am loved until the love is as pain, as a scourge of whips on my lover's back, as a fire that torments and consumes my lover.' Blessed is this lover that torments day and night, night & day, for it also illumines and sustains when the loved one is kind – be kind, then, my Soulina.

Your John

                               The Love That Dares

Djuna Barnes
(1892–1982)

The artist and novelist Djuna Barnes wrote *Ladies Almanack* (1928), a 'bawdy satire' on the lesbians in Natalie Clifford Barney's coterie (see page 77), at Barney's suggestion. Barnes is probably best known today for her novel *Nightwood* (1936), which also features a lesbian narrative and is considered a seminal modernist text. When asked about her own sexuality, Barnes famously said, 'I'm not a lesbian, I just loved Thelma.'

Thelma Wood (1901–70) was, like Barnes, an American expat living in Paris in the 1920s, having moved there to study sculpture. As was true of many others, their relationship was intense and unbalanced: though they both had affairs, Barnes wanted monogamy while Wood preferred polyamory. Eventually their relationship ended when Wood fell in love with Henriette Metcalf (1888–1981) sometime in 1928. *Nightwood* is a fictionalized account of Barnes's relationship with Wood. In the letter below to her friend Emily Coleman (1899–1974), Barnes recalls the relationship.

November 22, 1935

111 Waverly Place
New York City

Emily dear: I am very distressed by your last two
letters. Your agony is such an ecstasy that I am really
nervous about writing you as you ask me to, to tell
you what I think. To begin with I must repeat that
I do not, and can not have your attitude toward
sex itself. I do not think it monstrous and evil. You
should not despise the key, which is what it is, to all
we ever really learn. Now, in your case it seems to
me, from what little I know of you, that in the sexual
direction you have been cruelly starved, certainly so in
your relations with Peter. Therefore that you should
flounder about and clutch at the merest straw is
certainly not wicked or immoral or any of those things
you call it. The fact that you can be in love with Peter
and yet turn to Leonard, and now to Barker is pretty
conclusive proof that there is something monstrously
lacking in your relations with Peter.

In any case I know from my experience with
Thelma, that no one could have thrown me into
any other arms, not even for the months when I had

nothing whatsoever to do with her, not even after we had separated for a number of years, how many? two? three? I simply had no room for any other 'terrible attraction', and that you have proves, it seems to me, that something is deadly missing.

[...]

That you are going to hurt Peter is probably true, but the fact that you blame yourself for not waiting for Barker, merely means that Peter is not your true love, or how can you say it? Yes, you should have been pretty sure about Peter, about making him a 'target forever', because he is as he is. But also his own character makes him, inevitably, a target, that is why he fought you so desperately. With T. and myself it was in this degree very different, she did not fight me, she wanted me (along with the rest of the world).

[...]

You can't, you simply can't, put sex out of life, it won't have it – it's a law of nature, and how sinful it is to follow that law, well, that is the individual's problem, according to his belief. I do not say you may not have been wrong in forcing Peter, perhaps you were. Perhaps he has a right to be lifted up and slain, it may be what he needs. You can't know the pattern of your history and fate until it has been committed ...

… I am having a beastly time myself, what with your news about my book, your news about yourself …

Last night my sweet brother (of course 'in fun', so charming!) said I was 'full of shit'. Thelma here yesterday (she's broke!) said she did not like William James' Variety of Religious Experience as it was superficial and proved him ignorant, even of his quotations from St. Augustine; St. Augustine believing that evil was not a substance, but a swerving from truth, that James thought good and evil two substances, etc, etc. She also said Gromaison's Life of Christ the best (I must admit I never heard of it, or if I have, don't recall it. Have you seen it?)

… Emily darling, I don't know what to do or to say to you in your trouble, and then too I write knowing that between writing and answer there are some twenty odd days in which heaven knows, anything or nothing can happen. You ask the impossible. When you ask me what makes you a child, if anyone knew the answer to that, the world would end. 'Can you help it that you do not grow up?' I do not believe so, Emily – tho knowing yourself a child is a long step.

Love & write at once

D.

Gluck
(1895–1978)

Born Hannah Gluckstein, the British painter Gluck rejected any first name or prefix, because they were gender-nonconforming. For a time part of the artists' colony based at Lamorna in Cornwall, Gluck was noted for their floral paintings and portraits. One of their best-known works is *Medallion* (1936), a combined self-portrait and portrait of Gluck's lover Nesta Obermer (1893–1984). Gluck and Nesta had gone to a production of Mozart's *Don Giovanni* at Glyndebourne on 23 June 1936. Sitting in the third row, Gluck reported that they had felt the intensity of the music fuse them into one person and match their love. This painting, which Gluck referred to as the 'YouWe' picture, was subsequently used on the cover of the 1982 Virago edition of Radclyffe Hall's *The Well of Loneliness* (see page 83).

[undated, autumn 1936]

My own darling wife. I have just driven back in a
sudden almost tropical downpour in keeping with
my feelings at leaving you – my divine sweetheart,
my love, my life. I felt so much I could hardly be
said to feel at all-almost numb and yet every nerve
ready to jump into sudden life. I made straight for
the studio and tried to be busy and have more or less
succeeded, except that everything seems so utterly
unimportant that isn't us or connected with us.

I am interested now only in you and my work,
a vast interest really and it doesn't leave time or
energy for anything else.

Dearest and Best – this brings you my love – my
hopes that you have a good journey and every
thought and wish for your happiness and health.
Take care of your darling self for your own Boy-ee's
sake – if not for your own. I love you with all my
being now and for ever. Good morning dear heart
and goodbye.

In bed, Thursday morning, 7 January (1937)

My one instinct was to fly backwards into
nothingness – no contacts, no heart, no feelings.
I was furious with myself having bothered to find
out what posts would reach you most quickly. What
did it matter – if you didn't get them at night next
morning would do.

Your mother was right, I ask too much – and yet
I do not ask what I am not prepared to do and give
myself ... You will never know the turmoil, the quite
cold blooded that seized me – rage, just the same rage
that I got at Plumpton when Seymour kept us both
hanging about and I did not know when you were
coming in to see me.

Don't make any mistake – I know you love me,
I know how you love me and I know that nothing
like this can prevent me loving you, but my ears
went back and I felt that armour close with a snap
again round my heart which had become, I suddenly
realised <u>dangerously</u> softened ...

I went to bed. There was nothing else to do – I
was sick with myself for minding at all. I had so
nearly reduced feeling to insensitiveness and now
I had let it get all vulnerable again. I determined

not to think about it and when in bed took Dial [a barbiturate – not the soap] and a purge and hoped by this morning I would find it was all exaggeration and a result of being overtired. At 3 am I woke up with the headache worse than ever and took two aspirin and slept till nine. I felt better and calmer but it would not be possible just the same not to write all this to you … You see darling, when you are near or with me, it's like a warmth that keeps me from analysing and retrospecting and gradually I melt and feel human and creative and happy and all the suspicions bred by my life so far just seem impersonal and of no account and are lulled and I am tamed and safe and happy in it. Then when something like this happens I can feel my ears go back, I can feel my jaw set, I can feel that overwhelming urge to fly – to the desert I know so well it would be, but it seems safe somehow …

I don't think with all this outpouring of words I have made it clear what I minded. I manage, and you manage, to keep some semblance of our true relationship going, but when you are the chattel, as far as your goings and comings are concerned, of someone else, then I become it too and that, at sudden moments like last night, becomes intolerable.

Do try to understand. I have understood all your very strong feelings about the clutching things in my life. I suppose it's just the old Adam pouring upward to my brain but you are the only human being I have ever trusted and therefore loved. I do love you and I know what your love is for me and it is true that you sustain my spirits but I am human after all and if what I have written is small and seems a fuss about nothing, don't forget that it is the tiny things that count and that try as one may to keep the big view they can buzz like gnats and be very disturbing.

How I wish to God I could say all this with you in my arms and your head snuggled on my shoulder. Having got it out I feel better and closer to you even though it's on paper and Heaven alone knows how and with what a mood you will read it. The sun is pouring into my room on to our bed. Mabel [Gluck's housekeeper] has just been in to see if I'm alright. I assured her I was grand and just getting up which I am.

One disadvantage of my job is that it shuts me up in one room and there is nothing to stop a bee buzzing, and to you, constantly on the move and with additional fresh contacts all this eremite drooling will seem exaggerated.

... All my love to you as ever – and for ever
That was only pale because I blotted it at once.
Not because I feel reticent about it. <u>All my love now</u>
<u>and forever.</u>

Sylvia Townsend Warner
(1893–1978)

Sylvia Townsend Warner and Valentine Ackland (1906–69) were both writers who, in addition to co-authoring a book of poetry, *Whether a Dove or a Seagull* (1933), were also lovers from 1930 to Ackland's death. Elizabeth Wade White moved to the UK in the late 1930s, telling her family she needed to travel to conduct research on the poet Anne Bradstreet, but also joining the American Friends Service Committee as a relief worker. She met fellow anti-fascists in Warner and Ackland.

White made several trips to Spain in 1937 and 1938, and always had Warner's and Ackland's support, often staying with them at their home in Dorset. In late 1938 White's mental health suffered and she spent that winter in Dorset with Warner and Ackland. The amicable dynamic between the three changed in December 1938, however, when Ackland and White took a trip for three days and nights to a friend's place in the woods called Rat's Barn.

The weather was bad but they didn't care – they hadn't travelled to sightsee anywhere other than the bedroom.

By 12 January 1939 Warner and Ackland were still sharing a house but Sylvia was sleeping in the spare room. As Peter Haring Judd writes in *The Akeing Heart* (2018):

> Valentine and Elizabeth shared the front room. Sylvia was often kept awake by Elizabeth's insistent efforts to convince Valentine to stay in America with her. What each of the women had hoped for did not come to be in 1939; Sylvia did not regain Valentine's undivided love; Valentine's passion for Elizabeth rested uneasily with her love for Sylvia; Elizabeth learned that Valentine would not fully commit to her.

White returned to the US, heartbroken that Ackland wouldn't leave Warner. For her part, Townsend Warner continued to take the high road while throwing some magnificent shade in response to a letter from White about her own sufferings in love.

... to Elizabeth Wade White

Frome Vauchurch
Maiden Newton, Dorset

19.x.1938

Dearest, always to be dear, Elizabeth.

I should like to think that we shall have met before this letter reaches you, but I must write at once.

Your letter and your telegram reached me this morning. I was out last night, so they could not telephone the wire. First of all, do not reproach yourself. It was fatality, not fault; and only one fatality, a single blackout, not anything in the true course of your star ... a finger of the cloud that moves over all of us. You are a casualty, as much of a casualty as any fighter cast on to a stretcher, whether you were hit in Paris, in Madrid, at Winterton, here, it is a flying splinter from the same bombardment. All these long days I have been cursing the delay that kept you on this rack. I didn't expect it, I didn't not expect it. But I knew what you were exposed to, and that such things as breaking-points are a matter of laws, of stresses and strains, that the mind is material as steel or timber in this matter.

Next, what your doctor said was absolutely true. And I praise you for the disciplined mind that was able to accept the verdict; it would have been so easy to go on a little further into the refuge of madness; and you did not, and that is mostly admirable, and something must stead you now.

And last, you must come here as soon as you feel fit to travel – or else you must send for me and we will come back together.

Try to cut out London if possible until you have been here. If it is not a matter of gear, Janet can see to it; and if it is a matter of formality, formalities can wait. When you see our river flowing so beautifully and our looks of true love you will – no, not forget, forgetfulness is idle, and you have an industrious mind – but you will know that life is a co-operation with living, and that you love life and are right to love it, and that the things that befall one have significance, are not the mere dead weight of catastrophe.

I think of you with unchanged love, I want with all my heart to see you here. I weep for you, but it is with compassion, not with pity. You have done nothing to add to the burden on our hearts, there is no such thing as disappointment or disillusion. You must believe this, or you would not love us as you do.

Always,

Sylvia

Warner was invited to the Third American Writers' Congress (which was held in New York) to speak about the threats to democracy Europe was facing at the time. She and Ackland stayed in the apartment White was sharing with a friend, while White herself was away in Washington, DC.

The letter that follows sees Ackland trying to appease White after a fight about her returning to the UK with Warner and not staying with White in the US.

The second letter from Ackland to White was written after Ackland had returned home to Dorset with Warner.

26 Jane Street, NYC

8.vi.1939

Dearest Elizabeth.

Washington; and the flat is full of your kindness
and Valentine has been showing me the things
you sent, but I have not yet grasped them enough
to write a proper thanks for them, because what is
first and chiefest on my mind is your letter. I wish I
knew the answer. A theory about suffering is not an
easy thing to have, one might as well have a theory
about cancer. That is to say, one at once admits its
existence, and desire to put it out of existence, and
suspects with considerable backing of evidence, that
a good deal of it, at any rate, could be abolished; but
never really knows how, for what works in one case
don't work in another, and so one is forced back
on that irritating half-truth that it is a question of
individual reactions. Some cats can swim and some
cats can't. But both as myself and as a Marxist – I
was myself first – I will not sit down on that half-
truth. There is more to it than individual reactions;
and the individual reaction of the sufferer is not the

only factor, one must also include the individual reaction of the person who tries to cure. I wish more people would realize this. In cancer they do. They blame the doctor, they don't say it is all their own wretched fault that the suffering can't be cured. In cancer we are more scientific.

Sometimes I think that the question of suffering is a question of partial adaptation. Say you have a long journey, and tight boots. The moment comes when by every physical good reason those boots should come off. But a moral sense (probably based on fear, since fear seems to be the basis of all morality) says: If you take off those boots you may never dare put them on again. And you have a journey to go. And so one endures the ills one has, rather than face the sharper complication which involves the antagonism of relief and after relief an extra effort; and the boots stay on; and limping and sore feet become elaborately identified with going a journey, instead of being identified, as they should be, with uncomfortable boots.

As you know, I am for taking the boots off. I am for the risk of being a hedonist, I think one should enjoy oneself exactly when and how one can, and be damned to the moment when the boots must be put on again. For one thing, one may be struck dead at any moment, and what a fool one would feel to die unhappier than one need be; and for another, every relaxation of emotional pain is a claim staked on happiness, either for oneself or for humanity. It seems to me that one is letting every one else down by being unhappy if one can possibly be anything else. It is marrying all one's daughters and granddaughters to a bad husband, just because one has married a bad husband oneself.

I suppose that is as far as I have a theory of suffering. It is a severe one because it makes one extremely skeptical towards the suffering of others. It obliges one to say, Need you have such sore feet instead of What sore feet you have. One does not deny the soreness of the feet (at least I hope I don't); but one does deny the obligation to keep on those boots.

I know you are unhappy, and have been, and have reason for being unhappy. But it seems to me also that you have had times when you need not be unhappy, when you have been with Valentine, which is our happiness; and that you have not made the most of those times; because you have tried to make of them more than the most. That is to say

you have tried to make a fine day into an insurance
against bad weather, you have thought more of what
it will be like when it is over than what it is like at
the time. And things are only what they are at the
time. There are no permanent moments. Whether
the clock the calendar or the dead knell end the
moment it is a thing that must end. There are no
roses that one can gather tomorrow.

Archibald MacLeish says the same thing about
poetry when he says: Poetry can not have an
elsewhere. He means that there can be no second
chance for a poem, no redeeming blood can make it
better than it is, no heaven can improve its rhyme-
schemes. It is unredeemable. Happiness can have
no elsewhere either. It is now or nowhere. The poet
knows this in his blood, he concentrates on getting
that poem as good as it can be. The person in love,
the person in lust, the person in pursuit of pleasure
must do the same thing – if he is not to be an
amateur.

I am certain you were not designed to be an
amateur in love. And if I say these things too you
it is exactly because I am treating you as a serious
artist. I have always treated you as a serious artist,
that is why you first liked me, that is why I now seem

to you at times extremely hard and unsympathetic. But it seems to me this. You have the quality to be a serious artist, in loving, in living; and you have been brought up to be an amateur. An amateur in love is a philanderer. All your training has been designed to minimize the serious sensuality of your character, to make you a philanderer in love instead of a serious lover. And this conflict between character and upbringing now edges you towards that blind alley way out (but it is not a way out, it is a way to the prison, the brothel or the convent) of being unhappy, of relaxing yourself into a frame of mind which says, as your letter says: 'There seems to be such an immensity of suffering, so much energy, so much potential happiness and accomplishment poisoned at the source and rotting into waste and expense of spirit.'

But if you would speak honestly out of yourself you should by now be able to say: 'Ackland, Valentine is coming on Friday.' Just that.

Can you bear an experiment? Try this. The next time you being to think of this cosmic suffering that makes an enormous cloudy shadow of your own black unit, analyse in yourself how much of that suffering really affects you; how much of it is a deepening of your own suffering, how much of it is on the other hand, a supporting, a sympathetic thought. How much of it, in fact, is really a thorn in your side and how much of it a trailing cloud of dark glory. You will find, for you are not a shallow person, that some of the suffering around you really and genuinely does make your unhappiness worse. But a lot of it doesn't. A lot of it either isn't there, or don't you know enough about it to establish its existence. In fact, you have been taking it on guess. And you have been taking it on guess because sorrow and *weltschmerz* come drowsily and soothe the wakeful anguish of the soul.

You see, I have come round to this. I am advising you not to soothe your anguish, in order to be happier, in order to have a stronger and more instantaneous hold on the joy that comes your way. It is not a council I would give to any one unless I respected them and their capacity to be more than an amateur.

> With my true love
> Sylvia

... from Valentine Ackland
to Elizabeth Wade White

It is late, my darling, & I am tired & very much disappointed & feeling as though all, here & in the world, were full of horror & dismay for us, with love gone & love most terribly going –

Later

I rang you up & heard you speak. I can't write now.

My whole heart, my mind, my body, all ache & beat with love for you, desire & love – love my darling – in pity's name tell me, all ways you can that you do love me & that you will love me! Tell me.

My darling,

Mark well this day, which is a Sunday and cold
at that, for on it I want to write you an important
question; perhaps a question second only in
importance to that first one of all – to which you so
certainly and beautifully answered 'Yes – I will'.

For many days now I have known that my need
for you was growing heavier and heavier, and I
have spent much time in wondering how possibly
things could be planned for us. I have come to some
decisions, discovered some certainties & suspect
that some other feelings which are at present
too confused to be counted upon will develop
themselves into certainties. Now it is of the utmost
importance for me to know from you exactly how
you feel about me, what you want for us, what you
would be willing and able to do.

We know enough now since you have been here
with me and seen the kind of life I have chosen

and prefer and since I have been with you in your country and seen some of your friends, something of your surroundings – We know enough of each other to realise that in many things we are very different and that there is conflict between our tastes, especially as regards people and social activities. It COULD be a most dangerous kind of conflict, and if we fought it out both of us would be bitterly maimed, I believe, and we would lose both love and respect for each other. Think of this, for I am sure it is true – You have already accused me of being unadaptable and unwilling to make small concessions; I'm troubled because I think you are right in saying that. I may manage to get better. There are obvious psychological reasons for my having become so, and I may manage to cure myself in part, anyway. But I DO NOT WANT to be wholly cured! I'm lazy enough as it is, and if I switched back again now to the kind of things I used so much to enjoy, I'd inevitably lose even the remnants of what I love even better, my darling, than anyone on the face of the earth. I could never promise you to become addicted to society! Mark that well.

Probably I could promise complete fidelity, because there is something beyond words precious to me in the very thing you have, sometimes, been ashamed of: your complete surrender to love, your generosity of giving, which puts it even beyond my capacity for doubt, so that even I believe quite easily that you do give me everything I can't explain to you, at this distance, how it is with me – but that quality above all others makes me unable to imagine me loving anyone else.

But fidelity of desire is not enough to give you, because what I would necessarily be asking from you is everything you have to give. And in return I could not offer you what is probably the most important thing of all, security. It's not only the dangers which, up to now, have naturally made you flinch: the intangible perils, like the word 'Mistress' with its implication of insecurity, irritability – Perhaps there is the important point: you could not face instability. If that is so, things are better – for you would not have to face any kind of instability.

You can see towards what these words lead: the future is so hazardous, especially on this day and in this month, and during this period of the world's history that we cannot foretell our fortunes at all, but we can and must confide to each other our hope. I love you Elizabeth, and I want you. And these are two perfectly direct statements of very simple and most powerful emotions. The complications come, as always, in the actual making-real of my wishes. But I am convinced beyond a doubt now that they must be made real. You will mis-judge me if you think I am being completely self-thinking in this; I wish I were. If I were we could, all three, be infinitely the better for it. But habit has got me down and I am unable to think for myself ALONE. That is where I am caught, and you with me. I am asking you, most desperately to help me now.

'I believe in you, I honour and revere and cherish you, and in all ways, for all my life, I love you. Keep that love safe and alive if you can, and think if you want to, of how it may be.'

That is what your latest letter says to me, and if I am right in reading that important word 'may' as a promise on your part – then, my deeply loved, I have a right to ask your help now in working out a definite plan for our joint future.

Tell me, Elizabeth, very clearly and with complete candour, what you will do. I have dealt candidly with you; I have told you how it is – how I am unwilling to give up Sylvia-whose companionship is both dear and necessary to me: how she is unhappy and, I feel,

cheated of what she most wants from me. I see great
unhappiness ahead for her and I flinch before it. I do
not think that I can deal so with her, and yet these
weeks have shown me clearly that your image lies in
my arms. You are wanting me and I am wanting you,
and when we are together we lie down and we are
happy. We have desecrated and violated that happiness
NOT so much in allowing ourselves to be parted as by
wasting the time we had together in useless, miserable
recriminations and repining. This remembrance
frightens me. I want you to understand this – it
frightens me very much because I am no means sure
that you would be satisfied under any circumstances
with what my changing, self-willed, melancholy moods
might bring you. And I know that I could not endure
for half a year, again, the torments of reproaches and
frustrations that I endured last year and this year.

Here is plain-speaking, dear heart; necessary
now as never before. You must endure it, if you
will, because of the whole of two lives' happiness at
stake. I am not trying to hurt you, nor am I trying
to reproach you or be severe with you. I love you so
desperately and so warmly that sometimes the flames
leap from me to you, and would you too. Remember,
if you can, that they bite into me all the time.

You will know from the newspapers that at
this moment I am writing we are expecting a
violent increase of pressure from Germany, and an
intensifying of the war. You know what that may
mean, if it happens, if we manage between us, you
and I, to make a plan of action, to arrange a method
of living so that we may be together and love and
care for each other (god knows it is a most difficult
thing to do, but my heart tells me we may do it –)
we are, even so, beset by these other dangers, and
they are many – sweetheart – as you know from our
conversations about probabilities. And money is
another danger: I can't conceivably get across the
Atlantic again, when the war stops, because the
crazy taxation has crippled my kind of income, and
there are no jobs for people like me … Lovers are
always fantastically hopeful, fantastically despairing,
fantastically lucky, and seemingly we have cause to
be all three!

You would have to leave (whether I were there
or you were here) very much that you enjoy and
love and have learned to count upon. Your life
(even if things work out so that it is what you think
you most entirely want) would be difficult and
hazardous. It would not, ever, be lonely or frustrated,

I believe, nor would it ever be poor in the things we both know to be what we want most. But it would demand from you an immense generosity, a measure of endurance (not endurance of me only – my sweetheart, but of other people – lack of other people – slights perhaps – and above all endurance of a state of reason dominating a state of feeling. This most difficult exercise –).

Would it be worth your while to sacrifice the affectionate approbation, the pampering, the praise and kindness of the people you have now; the comfort and assurance of being among them, the easy indulgence of your desires as whims, of your beliefs as fancies – and change to the CONFUSION of being so demandingly beloved, of being relied on, of being in all things treated as someone of first & real importance? For god's sake, think carefully about this. It is a most drastic change.

The alternative solution to the as-yet-unfound one I hope for is that we take whatever possible chances offer of being happy whenever we possibly can: that we continue in this miserable state of longing and wishing and hoping, that we try to stay true, that we tacitly allow ourselves to think of being false, that we take every chance of lesser

happiness that offers itself and try our separate
bests not to be crippled for ever by the weight of
our separate desires. It is NOT a hopeless situation,
this alternative one; it could be fairly fruitful of
contentment and richness. But your letters make
it clear that I have a simple want which cannot be
simply attained. I want you.

Keep this letter privately and read it carefully. I
ask you most earnestly not to discuss it with anyone
else at all, but to have it in your own mind, against
your own heart, before your own judgment only
– and then to write to me as simply and truthfully
as you can, giving me what hope, what help you
can, telling me if you love me and in what manner
you love me, if you would come to me, when that is
possible, and in what way, under what conditions,
you would come to me. Tell me any plans that may
have formulated themselves in your mind during
these long weeks, and what chances you think there
are of our being together.

As I explained to you before (I'm afraid it was
rather a brusque letter. It did NOT MEAN to be. I
tried hard to write straight-forwardly and so that it
was easy to understand, but the situation itself is so
immeasurably complicated) it is not now possible for

us to live all three together again. And I think Sylvia is right, and I am every day more sure that we could not manage it. So what?

Lastly: don't think I am whining. I chose to return here and I am not complaining about it. I was right to come. I think proved right in the event but certainly right in the prospect. But I did NOT choose to leave you, and I don't intend to lose you. I trust your assurances and I believe that we are matched in love. This being so – my heart breaks because you are not with me, because my arms are not holding you, because night comes and then day comes, and you are not beside me. And I send you this letter in love and truth and trust – answer it as soon as you can, as truthfully and carefully and fully as you can. And love me, always, and in every way.

Valentine

[Longhand]

And late on this same night, dear heart

One thing I've not managed to say which is much, much more important than any other thing: that if only we can together work out a means of being in love together, leisurely & jointly & securely, I will give you all in my power, of love & truth & care & protection & support & comfort & understanding: very much more, my lovely & beloved, than ever you have had – in fact & in hope I will guard you & cherish you, compel you & stay you – I will love you always and be true & strong for you always.

In between I shall ask you for just measure of truth, compliance and kindness – kindness & passion & surrender, some times of will. With love always & reproach for old wounds never – The same to be my agreement with you: love always, old reproaches never.

Lovers' enmity makes hard terms in conference, sweetheart! But can we resolve these ways & find a just & lasting peace between us? – Try. It is frighteningly difficult, but within & without we are beset. But I love you.

I think of your hair, your eyes, your hands, your body – I remember – I love you.

The Love That Dares

Benjamin Britten
(1913–1976)
&
Peter Pears
(1910–1986)

The composer Benjamin Britten lived openly with his partner, the tenor Peter Pears, at their home in Aldeburgh, Suffolk, for almost forty years. Britten wrote many pieces for Pears, including song cycles such as *Seven Sonnets of Michelangelo* and operas such as *Peter Grimes*.

Pears's work took him away from Britten for large periods of time. The couple's letters, covering the period 1942–75, reflect their deep love and attachment, while also being filled with more mundane matters about daily life and work that convey their convivial domesticity and 'everyday intimacy'. The first few reprinted here are from early on in their relationship; the final two are from near the end of Britten's life, when he was suffering from heart disease and Pears was still performing at venues across the globe.

... Peter to Benjamin

In the train
[? 23 November 1942]

My beloved darling –

I've just left you & we haven't started yet – I have
to write down again just what you mean to me – You
are so sweet taking all the blame for our miserable
tiffs, our awful nagging heart-aches – but I know as
well as I know anything that it is really <u>my</u> fault. I
don't love you enough, I don't try to understand you
enough, I'm not Christian enough – You are <u>part of
me</u>, and I get cross with you and treat you horribly
and then feel as if I could die of hurt, and then I
realise why I feel so hurt and aching – It's because
you are part of me and when I hurt and wound you,
I lacerate my very self ... I do love you so, my darling
– Even these quarrels & agonies have their uses –
They make me love you all the more –

Goodnight, my darling boy –

I kiss you
P.

... Benjamin to Peter

Friston Field, East Dean,
Nr Eastbourne, Sussex

[? December 1942]

My darling man,

Eth[1] is just going off to the post; I hadn't realised that
it went so early, – so this has can only be a scribble,
to say how your letters have been life & breath to
me. My darling – to think I have been so selfish as to
make you unhappy, when you have so much strain,
& such hard work to bear. But I too have come out
of this week-end a better person. I seem to be getting
things into order abit. Again it seems to be a matter
of 'O man, know thyself' – & of knowing what I
really want – & living that knowledge. I promise, my
darling ...

It is lovely being here. You must come soon &
consumate it. Eth is an angel, & I think I make her
very happy coming. We talk always about you.

1   Ethel Bridge, wife of composer Frank Bridge, whom Britten was visiting.

I don't think the maisonette that I saw yesterday
will do – too far away & too many rooms & abit
gloomy. But we can go & look again on Saturday.
I called you last night, but you were already out,
I'm afraid. I'll try again to-morrow night.

Meantime – I live for Friday, & you. My man –
my beloved man.

B.

… Peter to Benjamin

Midland Hotel
[early December 1942]

My boy – It was such heaven hearing your voice –
I woke up again at once – I'd been wiling away the
time re-reading Mr Norris of which I've found a
Penguin [this refers to a Penguin paperback edition
of Christopher Isherwood's novel *Mr Norris Changes
Trains* (1935)].

You know, I've been thinking an awful lot about
you and me – I love you with my whole being,
solemnly and seriously – These last times have
made me realise how serious love is, what a great
responsibility and what a sharing of personalities

– It's not just a pleasure & a self indulgence. Our
love must be complete and a creation in itself, a gift
which we must be fully conscious of & responsible
for.

O my precious darling, parting from you is such
agony – Just hearing your voice is joy –

Goodnight, my Ben –

Sleep well, I shall think of you all the time –

> Your loving man
> P.
> Lots of love to Eth.

[letterhead: Midland Hotel, Birmingham]
[after November 1942]

My beloved darling, my little pussy-cat –

This is only really to tell you (probably all in vain
because you won't get it – and you'll leave just as the
post arrives!) that I love you and miss you terribly –
Every loving couple I see I envy – I go to the movies
and weep buckets because every situation I translate
to our personal one. Oh! I do hope we'll never be in
quite such a dilemma as Humphrey Bogart & Ingrid
Bergman get themselves into in 'Casablanca'; promise
me that you won't leave me just as the Nazis enter
London because you hear your husband isn't dead
after all, and then turn up with him at the speakeasy
I'm running in Newfoundland, trying to forget you –
promise me, you won't, will you? For one thing, I'm
sure I should never behave as nobly as Bogart does!
Bee!
    Look, I've got to rehearse a little while here on
Friday Morning 10.30–11.30 or so, so I shan't be
back in town until the afternoon – See you then –
                    Love! Love! Love.
                    P. xxxooo etc.

... Benjamin to Peter

Old Mill, Snape
[6 April 1943]

My darling,

This is not a real letter – you know what little
news there is – but only a Coda to our inevitably
emotionally-restricted telephone talks. I love you, my
only one, & think of you every moment – my life is
inextricably bound up in yours, & so I wonder every
moment exactly what you are doing – how Rigoletto
is going how you are managing to get to Hull &
back, whether you are too exhausted to sing at all –
& ~~all~~, etc. etc. I can't wait till I see you – don't think
because I demurred a little at coming on Thursday,
~~be a~~ that I am not every bit as excited as you are, but
I'd got it into my silly head that you were only back
on Friday, & had made arrangements accordingly
(Iris is coming up with me) – but, it is all settled, &
I'll tell you details on the telephone. You poor dear,
when <u>are</u> you going to get a little time to rest &
relax? ...

Until Thursday, all my love.
B.

My darling heart (perhaps an unfortunate phrase –
but I can't use any other) I feel I must write a squiggle
which I couldn't say on the telephone without
bursting into those silly tears – I do love you so
terribly, & not only glorious you, but your singing.
I've just listened to a re-broadcast of Winter Words
(something like Sept. '72) and honestly you are the
greatest artist that ever was – every nuance, subtle &
never over-done – those great words, so sad & wise,
painted for one, that heavenly sound you make, full
but always coloured for words & music. What have I
done to deserve such an artist and man to write for?
I had to switch off before the folk songs because I
couldn't anything after – 'how long, how long'. How
long? – only til Dec. 20th – I think I can just bear it
    But I love you,
    I love you,
               I love you – B.

P.S. The Folk Song Suite ('Up she goes'?) is just
finished – good I hope.

... Peter to Benjamin

[postmark 21 Nov 1974]

My dearest darling

No one has ever ever had a lovelier letter than the
one which came from you today – You say things
which turn my heart over with love and pride,
and I love you for every single word you write.
But you know, Love is blind – and what your dear
eyes do not see is that it is you who have given me
everything, right from the beginning, from yourself
in Grand Rapids! through Grimes & Serenade
& Michelangelo and Canticles – one thing after
another, right up to this great Aschenbach – I am
here as your mouthpiece and I live in your music –
And I can never be thankful enough to you and to
Fate for all the heavenly joy we have had together
for 35 years.

My darling, I love you – P.

Bad Gays

In their excellent podcast *Bad Gays*, hosts Huw Lemmey and Ben Miller take a forensic look at the warts-and-all lives of LGBTQ+ icons past and present. In an episode on Benjamin Britten (10 November 2020), they talk with John Bridcut, who interviewed several men for his book *Britten's Children*. These men, now elderly, were taken under Britten's wing as young boys, performing in several of his works, including *Peter Grimes*. While there was never anything sexual about Britten's attentions – he seems, in fact, to have valued these boys for the licence they gave him to be childlike, a fellow child with them – what they recount with pain is the way Britten would drop them, immediately, once they hit puberty, leaving them sad and confused about what they could have done to lose his friendship and affection. We recommend the book – and the podcast – for their clear-eyed view of the complexities not just of Britten but of all the LGBTQ+ people they discuss.

The Love That Dares

John Cage
(1912–1992)

The composer John Cage first met the dancer and choreographer Merce Cunningham (1919–2009) in the late 1930s. At the time John Cage was married to the painter and sculptor Xenia (née Kashevaroff, 1913–95), but when he met Merce again in 1942 in Chicago, they began an affair. John divorced his wife in 1945, and he and Merce lived together for the next forty-seven years.

The letters from John to Merce reprinted below are taken from the first heady days of their relationship.

[undated, postmarked July 7, 1943]

550 Hudson St., New York

Lover:

Now in dark of 2nd week; look like battled and
scarred person (mostly from fatal weekend in N.J.,
country not seeming to agree with me unless you are
there): a boil, 50,000,000 bites and blisters, general
debility.

Two letters from you (one at home + one at
library), and I, glad that the translation business
interests you: will send new article presently.

This morning all the parts of me that haven't
heard that you are away got me up and out early and
longing to lie down beside you.

Country had a special moment when your spirit
reached me in a leafy place and made embrace.
Would love to share with you if even pigtail.
The trivia people may have tangents that you
will luminesce if you get close enough, like dead
(otherwise) tubes brought into electric atmosphere.

I love the peace and beauty and absence of elegance connoisseurs. Your words paint idyll land.

Love you,

J.

Starved for good long fuck with you.

Postscripts:

Thought you'd be amused to know that Dad's newest inhalation medicine is designed to increase the male's resistance to orgasm.

Maybe you're angry or disgusted because I write too full of desire and getting sexy.

They are taking down the Enemy display. Passing by, saw 'S THIS FOR YOU.'

Make me a dance that is a sex love dance, sans frustration.

I am in oestrus now thinking of you – such a full-fledged need.

[undated, postmarked July 22, 1944]

12 E. 17th St., New York

[This letter is intentionally cut in various places, and
it is also typewritten on the page both horizontally
and vertically, as indicated below.]

[horizontal]
today is beautiful and I am dreaming of you and
enigma [John's nickname for Merce's penis] and how
we are together today: your words in my ears making
[me] limp and taut by turns with delight. oh, I am
sure we could use each other today.

    i like to believe that you are writing my music
now: god knows i'm not doing it, because it simply
seems to happen. the prestissimo is incredible the
way you are and is perhaps a description and song
about you.

    banalities: blue check arrived and dv et Helmsley
got theirs; i am afflicted with bills of all description,
but do not seem to be able to be sensible about
money. passed by clyde's yesterday with their
socks; they look beautiful. had, for a change, a
pleasant time with Schuyler [Chapin, impresario

and producer]; he informs me that Oliver [Smith, set designer] who called the other day and wanted to know whether you could hold a tune and what kind of voice you had, with Robbins [Jerome, theatre director, producer, choreographer], has you in mind for the lead of their dance-musical; it doesn't mean you have to sing like galli-curci, but like American sailor[s] sing (and see stripes au meme temps?)

there is apparently a part in the book where you would go through a tunnel of love and everyone thinks you would do it very well: so do i, please go through mine, taking your time, if you will.

also schuyler had evening with virgil [Thompson, composer] and v.t. now says i am ultra-genius, having seen some of 2 piano work, and that i am on a par with picasso, schoenberg, stravinsky, satie, matisse, cezanne, van gogh etc. ad nauseum: schuyler now thinks virgil had good reasons for not reviewing other concerts, will blare next one to skies, that his review of it is really already written, that he has been making careful decisions about what to say etc. i don't like being great. it's not good for my relation with calliope, who by the way, is not female, and looks exactly like you.

pardon the intrusion: but when in september will

you be back? i would like to measure my breath in relation to the air between us.

[vertical]

in one letter i said absurd things about inexpressivity; obviously wrong, but what i meant was that high expressivity often comes about through no attempt to make it or to express anything. had dinner one night with denby [Edwin, dance critic]; i think he's a sad little man who's frightened of something. read his poetry which has some good qualities, but is by no means off this earth. i keep reading marvelous myths in joe [Campbell]'s book, but joe, too, is not really fine fine writer. of course, this is first draft i have and he will probably improve it. would you like me to send copy of finnegan[s Wake, by James Joyce] book which is out now or would you rather save that for home-reading?

need you deliciously.

gas bill came but is nothing; do not worry about it.

prestissimo will be complex at first, then simple then complex and then faster yet to end entire piece which should be finished in two weeks, because have more things to write; i am so happy with this music

that i shall be sad when it is all written. each sound
has gotten to be friendly and something i know and
have pleasure with; they are so well trained, too.

send me some little twig or a hair from near
enigma or a piece of grass that you touched and
sunbathed with, mon prince.

Bayard Rustin
(1912–1987)

Bayard Rustin was both an American civil rights activist, working alongside Dr Martin Luther King Jr, and a leader in other political and social movements, including socialism, non-violence and gay rights.

An openly gay man in the fiercely homophobic times of the early 1960s, he was on many occasions attacked, arrested and dismissed from important leadership positions. In spite of attempts to silence him, Rustin successfully helped to organize the Southern Christian Leadership Conference and Dr King's March on Washington for Jobs and Freedom. Criticism over his sexuality led to his taking a behind-the-scenes role, but he was nevertheless an influential adviser to civil rights leaders. In the 1980s he became a public advocate on behalf of gay causes, speaking at events as an activist and supporter of human rights.

The first letter is to his lover Davis Platt, whom Rustin had met in 1943. Platt and Rustin lived together as a couple in New York City after the Second World War. Rustin refers to Platt as 'Marie' or 'M.' in their letters.

The second letter is to John Swomley (1915–2010), a fellow activist, friend and founder member of the Fellowship of Reconciliation (FOR), at a time when Rustin had been arrested for an 'act of sexual perversion' and charged with lewd vagrancy.

... to Davis Platt

April 20, 1945

Dear Davis,

[...]

If I had now to make a final, but definitely final, decision on the basis of my present emotional propensity, it would be toward M. The reason for this is explained I believe by the nature of love itself. Love, as we have agreed, develops from shared experiences, a growing together. Between me and M. there has been since October a series of experiences that represent less fear, less deceit, and more understanding than between me and any other human with whom there has been any love indications. It came about gradually in letters, little acts of thoughtfulness, real criticisms that she made that I knew hurt her to make and which were for good and growth, and her loyalty at a time when most people suffering as she suffered would have run wildly in another direction for self-protection ...

Now the experience in the North Phila. Station must be seen in light of a real longing over months of struggle for a similar experience with someone like H[elen Winnemore]. (Here again I digress to say that for months I have felt that one's greatest problem in these matters is lack of confidence in one's self – fear – so it is natural that one should long for some little hope by way of an opening experience. I hope this last sentence makes sense. I can't say it any more clearly under the circumstances.) Now, there had been in the recent past no such … experiences with anyone like Helen. Fear, shame, deceit, and anxiety had so distorted relationships that even when I attempted on several occasions to talk with Doris about it all, I was blocked and bound. Then, Davis, suddenly for the first time in years H. and I together pushed open a door long closed. I suppose it was because she led me to tell her all (the very worst and much I had never had courage to discuss with a woman) that the door was opened a little when fear had fled and when a degree of mutual confidence took hold. Can you appreciate that something occurred in that moment that had not existed between me and a woman since Nonie years ago? Then, add my vast desire for such a contact and perhaps you will better sense what took place – a leading – a sincere, seriously selfless one

The Love That Dares

– a confession – then a joy that is almost beyond understanding – a flash of light in the right direction – a new hope, ever so small by comparison, but it was there – then a sudden revelation …

If I can't depend on you and A.J. [Muste], on whom can I depend? For I know, as Paul knew, my poor will is not enough; for that I would do, I do not; and that I would not do, I do. I know also that I tend to be a person of action and that I often act when emotionally aroused and thus act hastily … without proper consideration. This is an unhealthy state and must be cut out. On the other hand (and this is not to justify hasty or ill-considered action), it is perhaps highly misleading and to a degree dishonest to make moment-to-moment decisions when one's mind and feelings are at battle and one is consequently in an unusually fluid and (I hope) growing state.

Any answer to M. will have in part to spring from what I finally am able to be – a thing I frankly am not certain of at the moment. It is not easy to remain here in a monosexual world and make progress. So much of our energy is taken in building up resistances for keeping the simple pledge of abstinence here. Sometimes I wonder if those outside can know the terrific tensions!

Let me go on, however, to recapitulate: 1) Emotionally, I am at present strongly attached to Marie; intellectually, I know that every effort must be made to find a different solution, for my vocation, which is my life, is at stake; 2) My relation to M., on one hand, is good in that it has been a real bulwark against looseness and fatigue in an emotionally trying monosexual existence ... My relation to M. is a problem, as A.J. pointed out when he said 'her very attachment to me might instill in me either desire or mere loyalty that would inhibit my attempts to take up H.'s way.' But here again how does one come to a decision? Is one inwardly ready to decide? Can a decision have meaning that does not grow into being? Are there times when one must simply cut oneself off? Does one weigh six against seven and come to a decision or does some inexplicable factor say 'there are only six on this side, but really this is the right side'? When I weigh, I see the power M. has exerted in helping me in holding the line. Is not this valuable, I say? But then I wonder, am I rationalizing in ... wanting to hold on? Is such dependence on a love object necessary? Can more prayer replace this apparent need? Can one strongly driven exist without a harness? If I abandon all thoughts of

Marie before another can take her place, am I
making a mistake? Or, indeed, is it possible? How can
I find such another in this abnormal world? Ought
I to abandon this world? Can I do that without
abandoning my principles? Is celibacy the answer? If
so, how can I develop an inner desire for it? I have
a real desire for following another way but I have
never had a desire to completely remove sex from
my mind. What can celibacy become without such
an inner drive? Does not holding M. before me as an
object toward whom I project these terrific impulses
stifle the beam of light I saw when I spoke with H.?

Sincerely your friend,
Bayard Rustin

... to John Swomley

March 8, 1953

Dear John,

Thank you for your kind letter and please forgive
my delay in answering. As you probably know by
now, we are quite limited in the number we can
write. In some ways your letter meant more to me
than many of the others I received – for it was a
very warm note that reveals that more sensitive side
of you that you should reveal more often – mostly
your other wonderful qualities if you would be a
really unique person. Thank you for your hope
and faith. In one way I was sorry to have to resign
from FOR because in the last year I had begun to
feel that the gulf that had existed between us was
just about bridged. You may not realize it (not your
fault but mine, likely) but I was really trying to work
more in the spirit of teamwork. In the past this
has not been easy for me for I have been very self-
centered and filled with pride. But I know that, in
God's way of turning ugliness and personal defeat
to triumph, I have gone deeper in the past six weeks

than ever before and feel that I have at last seen my real problem. It has been pride in self. In most of the dramatic ways, the so-called big ways, I was prepared to give all. I would, I believe, have died rather than join the army. But in the small and really primary ways I was as selfish as a child. I am sure that in a way I must have known this. Now I feel it and know that pride must be overcome. No matter where I work in future, where I live and with whom I am, I have pledged before God that I will love more nonviolently in the small ways that support the big ones if they are to be real. While sex is a very real problem and while it has colored my personality, I know that it has never been my basic problem.

I know now that for me sex must be sublimated if I am to live with myself and in this world longer. For it would be better to be dead than to do worse than those I have denounced from the platform as murderers. Violence is not as bad as violence + hypocrisy. I have been reading the papers – alas, how mad we become. But I know now that men really do not 'feel' what they do. I know also that I have never been good enough to make them feel, really. So no matter where I am in the future, John, I shall always feel a certain closeness to you – a closeness that has grown from strife reconciled. When you pray – think of me. For in the new life I shall need more prayer and love than before. I trust you will not dismiss this letter as coming from the Bayard you have known, for God's mercy has permitted something new to be added.

All my love to those in the office. Special affection I send A.J., who does not realize that his love has kept me from going lower than I have, and whose everlasting faith has accompanied me through hell.

In fellowship,

Bayard Rustin

Lorraine Hansberry
(1930–1965)

The playwright Lorraine Hansberry was the first woman of colour to have a play, *A Raisin in the Sun*, performed on Broadway, and was the youngest playwright, at age twenty-nine, to win the New York Drama Critics' Circle Award. Her other plays include *Les Blancs*, but her career was cut short when she died tragically young, of pancreatic cancer, aged just thirty-four.

Born in Chicago to activist parents who had in 1940 brought a case before the US Supreme Court (*Hansberry v Lee*, which successfully challenged a racially restrictive covenant that barred African Americans from purchasing or leasing land in part of Chicago's Woodland neighbourhood), Hansberry moved to New York in 1950 and worked at the Pan-Africanist journal *Freedom*. There she wrote about the struggles of African nations for liberation and also about the oppression of gay men and lesbians. In 1953 she married the activist, publisher and songwriter Robert B. Nemiroff; they separated in 1957 and divorced in 1962.

Never openly gay, Hansberry wrote the letter included here (published in May 1957) to *The Ladder*, a magazine produced by the lesbian-rights organization Daughters of Bilitis, which Hansberry had joined that year. In it she expresses her gratitude that a forum like theirs exists for lesbians.

I'm glad as heck that you exist. You are obviously serious people and I feel that women, without wishing to foster any strict separatist notions, homo or hetero, indeed have a need for their own publications and organizations. Our problems, our experiences as women are profoundly unique as compared to the other half of the human race. Women, like other oppressed groups of one kind! or another, have particularly had to pay a price for the intellectual impoverishment that the second class status imposed on us for centuries created and sustained. Thus, I feel that THE LADDER is a fine, elementary step in a rewarding direction.

Rightly or wrongly (in view of some of the thought provoking discussions I have seen elsewhere in a homosexual publication) I could not help but be encouraged and relieved by one of the almost subsidiary points under Point 1 of your declaration of purpose, '(to advocate) a mode of behaviour and dress acceptable to society'. As one raised in a cultural experience (I am a Negro) where those within were and are forever lecturing to their fellows about how to appear acceptable to the dominant social group, I know something about the shallowness of such a view as an end in itself.

The most splendid argument is simple and to the point, Ralph Bunche, with all his clean fingernails, degree's, and, of course, undeniable service to the human race, could still be insulted, denied a hotel room or meal in many parts of our country. (Not to mention the possibility of being lynched on a lonely Georgia road for perhaps having demanded a glass of water in the wrong place.)

What ought to be clear is that one is oppressed or discriminated against because one is different, not 'wrong' or 'bad' somehow. This is perhaps the bitterest of the entire pill. HOWEVER, as a matter of facility, of expediency, one has to take a critical view of revolutionary attitudes which in spite of the BASIC truth I have mentioned above, may tend to aggravate the problems of a group.

I have long since passed that period when I felt personal discomfort at the sight of an ill-dressed or illiterate Negro. Social awareness has taught me where to lay the blame. Someday, I expect, the 'discreet' Lesbian will not turn her head on the streets at the sight of the 'butch' strolling hand in hand with her friend in their trousers and definitive haircuts. But for the moment, it still disturbs. It creates an impossible area for discussion with one's most enlightened (to use a hopeful term) heterosexual friends. Thus, I agree with the inclusion of that point in your declaration to the degree of wanting to comment on it.

I am impressed by the general tone of your articles. The most serious fault being at this juncture that there simply is too little.

Would it be presumptuous or far-fetched to suggest that you try for some overseas communications? One hears so much of publications and organizations devoted to homosexuality and homosexuals in Europe; but as far as I can gather these seem to lean heavily toward male questions and interests.

Just a little afterthought: considering Mattachine; Bilitis, ONE; all seem to be cropping up on the West Coast rather than here where a vigorous and active gay set almost bump one another off the streets – what is it in the air out there? Pioneers still? Or a tougher circumstance which inspires battle? Would like to hear speculation, light-hearted or otherwise.

L.H.N., New York, N.Y.

Allen Ginsberg
(1926–1997)

The poet Allen Ginsberg, best known for his poems
Howl and *Kaddish*, was one of the 'Beat' group of
writers and artists in 1950s and 1960s San Francisco
which included Lawrence Ferlinghetti, Gregory Corso,
William S Burroughs and Jack Kerouac. These artists'
work expressed the dissatisfactions and activism of the
post-Second World War generation. Ginsberg was a
passionate and gifted performance poet, but his work
was often controversial at the time – *Howl* was the
focus of an obscenity trial that ultimately led to changes
in US publishing laws. He was a significant figure of
the counterculture movement and its reaction against
capitalism, militarism and sexual repression. Ginsberg
met Peter Orlovsky (1933–2010) in San Francisco in
1954. Peter was working as an artist's model for the
painter Robert La Vigne. Allen was living with a girlfriend,
with whom Peter was also having a sexual relationship

at the time. Theirs remained an open relationship: Peter, who was bisexual, continued to have relationships with both men and women throughout their 43 years together.

The letters from Allen to Peter included here are from a period when they were separated, Allen having left California first for India and then Paris. Peter joined him there in 1957 and, with Ginsberg's encouragement, began to write poetry of his own. They lived in a lodging house above a bar at 9 rue Gît-le-Coeur which came to be known as 'the Beat Hotel'. Gregory Corso was already living there, and soon they were joined by William S Burroughs. Ginsberg began his epic poem 'Kaddish' there; Corso composed *Bomb* and *Marriage*; Burroughs (with help from Ginsberg and Corso) put together his work *Naked Lunch* from earlier attempts. The photographer Harold Chapman also lived there for a time, and documented this period in his photographs. The 'hotel' closed in 1963.

Allen and Peter remained together in what they referred to as 'a marriage sealed by vows' until Ginsberg passed away in 1997.

Dear Peter,

Got your letter yesterday, was so happy to receive
it and your sweet sex talk. I ... was longing for kind
words from heaven which you wrote, came as fresh
as a summer breeze & 'when
I think on thee dear friend / all losses are restored
& sorrows end' came over & over in my mind – it's
the end of a Shakespeare Sonnet [30] – he must have
been happy in love too. I had never realised that
before ... Write me soon baby, I'll write you big long
poem I feel as if you were god that I pray to –

Allen Ginsberg

I'm making it all right here, but I miss you, your arms & nakedness & holding each other – life seems emptier without you, the soul warmth isn't around ...

The Animals

The writer Christopher Isherwood (*A Single Man*, etc.) and Don Bachardy were together for thirty years, having met on the beach in Santa Monica, California, in 1952. They were painted by David Hockney in 1968 and were the subjects of a moving documentary, *Chris & Don*, in 2007. In 2020 their correspondence were the basis of an eleven-episode podcast entitled *The Animals: A Love Story Told in Letters*, performed by Simon Callow and Alan Cumming, together with writer and scholar Katherine Bucknell. The title of the podcast comes from the couple's names for themselves: 'Dobbin', the stubborn workhorse, was Isherwood; 'Kitty', the playful feline, was Bachardy.

John Dalby
(1929–2017)
&
John Thompson
(1924–2018)

John Dalby was a British actor, singer, composer and musician. Born in Bristol, he attended the Bristol Old Vic Theatre School and the Guildhall School for Music and Drama and appeared in many roles on stage and screen. He also worked behind the scenes as a composer, most notably perhaps for the 1984 film *A Passage to India*, in which he had a cameo role. Dalby also taught singing at the London School of Music and Dramatic Art and at the Actors' Richmond Centre. He was a dear friend to many in the music and theatre industry. Upon his death he left his partner of fifty-seven years, John Thompson.

These letters between the two Johns are taken from the very beginning of their relationship, when such a union was still a crime and these letters could have been used as evidence in any criminal case brought against them.

Dalby to Thompson

John Thompson, Esq
Clare Hall Hospital
South Mimms,
Barnet. Herts.

27 Elvaston Place
London SW7
Sep 15th 1960

My dear,

Sitting ruminating on the name Johnny (a name
I have always found repugnant when applied to
myself) and debating whether it is an affectionate
version of John or a diminutive of it, I wonder
whether you should be called Little John. You might
not favour this because, I remember your height is
a sore point with you and I do not want to rub salt
into the wound.

Nevertheless, the fact that you are physically
so small but big in so many other respects is an
enchantment for me and makes my fondness for you
unbounded.

John

27, Elvaston Place,
London S.W.7.

Mar 22nd '61.

My dear Littlelegs,

I have been meaning to write to you for some time
but as I saw you so often, the idea seemed absurd.
Now, as I haven't seen you for ages, the time has
come and it is sheer coincidence that you will get this
letter on <u>our</u> day!

Of course, I can't think of anything to say except
to reassure you that you have an indispensable part
of my life so I hope this suits you.

I really am grateful for all that you do for me, and
for others, for that matter; but apart from that it is
your sweet self I most admire and you give me much
happiness. I only hope that I give you some small
return.

Bien affecteusement

Yours

John

Thompson to Dalby

John Dalby Esq.
'Stage Door'
The Pavilion Theatre
Filey
Yorks.

Sunday. 18th June '61.

My Dearest.

A note to enquire after your welfare. I do hope
you are well and happy. I've just returned from my
weekend off and missed you so much. I went over
to 27 on Friday evening after having a few drinks
with Victor and one or two others at the Boltons.
I saw Anne and John ... I was a bit cross with Jon
as he greeted me with Hello have you heard from
Dalby, hasn't sent me any money yet. I'm afraid I
gave him a piece of my mind and let him know that
at least you were working and he'd get his money
(cheek). Anyway darling ... he was as nice as pie
on Saturday and had quite a romp in the kitchen
making coffee and things so don't worry. Try and

The Love That Dares

enjoy yourself and make the best of things up there.
I woke up on Saturday morning very early and kicked
a leg out, then an arm but realized how empty and
big the bed was without you needless to say I didn't
sleep a wink after-wards so decided to get up and do
some SORTING OUT! my dear, I've brought the
rest of your dirties home here to wash and iron and
I intend bringing back the bedspread to do, it will
need machinery round first then with the machine,
I hope you don't mind I shall eventually collect the
laundry…and put it away. What sort of polish should
I use on the piano? By the way there were two very
old and torn shirts so I've thrown them away (about
time)

… had lunch at South Ken then went in to see
Eileen, she was a bit put out because I'd had lunch,
telling me firmly that I should know she always got
lunch on Saturday, and that she [dusted] and made
the bed first then for lunch for us, any way I arrived
at 1-30 and left eventually at 5 after a good natter
and a laugh or two

She told me all about [J's] T.V. and how she was
there all day covered in sh—t from the cow or
something. I'm very pleased she managed to get some
work at last …

Last night we went to one or two clubs and then coffee at Leon's, who incidentally sens his love to you and best wishes. I saw Douglas who turned his nose up at me because I suppose Robin and one or two others were making a bit of a fuss he walked right past us, wearing tight blue jeans, a frightful shirt and looking not quite so attractive as before. still perhaps he was shy or didn't want to know us.

I received a large booklet for Filey Council offices today with holiday accommodations and agents for flats and things. according to this one should have no difficulty in finding a place suitable for us to share.

would you call in the office and ask for a Booklet. its called 'Filey Yorkshire Paradise'!!!

There are two separate agents for furnished flats. perhaps you might like to call on them …

Now I must close pet and get some work done. I did tell you of course that I shall be on holiday from Sunday 16th for two weeks. Unless the situation improves and I can have the three weeks together as planned so if you do book anything in advance remember the 16th.

I hope I haven't bored you darling. I love you very much. write soon.

J.

John Dalby Esq.
ᶜ/o 44 Clarence Drive
Filey
Yorks.

[postmarked 3 July 1961]

Same Address
Sunday. pm.

Mr Dearest.

Many thanks for your letter I waited to write
tonight as I thought I would have more to tell
you The weather has been wonderful until today
when we had a very sultry morning then rain all
afternoon since. however the few days before were
absolutely glorious and I was able to get a lot of
sunbathing done.

I collected to snaps on Friday and realized that
the B'pool snaps are still in the camera. So I suppose
we shall finish that one when I come up to GIley.
Sorry you had to work so hard last week darling but
never mind lots of pennies to spend on holiday!!!

Yesterday we went swimming and had a glorious

time it was so hot and the sun was glorious but unfortunately a young boy was drowned and it seemed to kill the excitement in everybody it was by that time about 5.30pm and the session was nearly over anyway. In the evening we went to a rather dull party at Richmond and it was so hot everyone was sweating it was like a Turkish bath so we left after about an hour and a half it was a relief to get out with the fresh air except that it was still very warm.

I took the bedspread in on Friday night and Anne looks wonderful she's slimmed and her hair is glorious all bouffant! and a lovely shade of light brown. J was more pleasant and they had a house full of guests Flick and others staying etc.

Did you have a nice chat to your Mum the other night, what did she say about her holiday, is she still not very keen. she has the notion that you will be going down to see her in B'ton, are you? I hope you can. At the moment I'm doing all sorts of peculiar times here, we all have had to do holiday relief and long days are absolutely killing especially during the hot weather. Anyway if won't be long before I'm on holiday myself and boy am I looking forward to it.

By the way I don't know how true the story goes but Anne told me that she thought Geraldine had

been trying to telephone me, it seems that she is
giving a dinner party or that she's invited Anne +
John over one evening, Anne isn't very keen on
going and why she should want to see me I'll never
know. Still we'll see what it's all about. Your mum
tells me that she is doing a course in Scarborough
with David Harshowe one weekend which is it do
you know? it will be a nice chance to see them both
again. darling it seems like years since you went away
and I feel as though I shall have to get to know you
all over again or at least thats the way it seems I
don't mind telling you I have a few tears when I saw
the snaps it was so nice to see your silly mug again.
Now I'd better close until tomorrow when I hope
there will be some sort of letter from you.

Monday morning

Your card to hand, how nice to hear from you again.
I do love you darling and count the hours when we
shall be together again. What a good idea having [J]
to stay it certainly will help out with the rent, but
whatever you do don't believe a word he tells you,
all has been left tidy excepting the hoover over the
floor and that each time I went was an impossibility,

it was always in use anyway I telephoned Anne and told her. evidently he has his own bed linen and he should be O.K. but of course he knows all about your place better than me!!!

I must close now and get back to the ward I've got nursing to do. Don't be too long writing that letter.

Lots of Love

J.

My Dearest John.

I've had your letter exactly 5 mins and as I'm off until 10.40 now is a good opportunity to write you again. Work is very hectic at the moment so I must sit down when I can.

Since I last wrote to you very little has happened except the fact that I went yesterday to see about a new car and was told to wait again until the Spring as the market for Second hand ones at the moment was bad and I would get a poor price for my present one. I'm very disappointed as I wanted to bring it up to Filey.

How dare you criticise my social record indeed. You can talk. I don't suppose you'll have time to even telephone me when you get back. I've played tennis, Swam in the new pool at [Halben] been to the Proms had a few meals out and gone to a couple of parties and thats all What about all these trips to the abbeys its sacrilege you heathen. perhaps you may come back just a little Spiritual! though.

Did Pat and Barry get my note? you didn't say, give them my love if not and tell them I'm longing to see them again.

What Mrs [Pank] show like, did it come over well, I'm pleased that Geraldine has made an impression on somebody, lets hope something comes of it.

Please do try and fix a date for coming back as I must know as soon as possible, be a love and try for little legs! I'm still crazy about you even though your corny, greying wrinkling and fart like thunder.

Love

John

Audre Lorde
(1934–1992)
&
Pat Parker
(1944–1989)

The poet and civil rights activist Audre Lorde grew up in New York, attending Hunter College High School (a school for intellectually gifted students, at that time all-girls), where a poem she submitted to the school literary journal was rejected, only to be accepted for publication by *Seventeen* magazine. After attending the National University of Mexico and Hunter College, and gaining a Master's degree in Library Science at Columbia University, she embarked on a career in letters, writing and teaching. She co-founded Kitchen Table: Women of Color Press, the first publisher for women of colour in the US, and became an associate of the Women's Institute for Freedom of the Press. From 1984 to 1992 she lived and worked in Berlin, having a profound effect on the women's movement there and increasing awareness of intersectionality.

Lorde met the poet Pat Parker (1944–89) in 1969 and they began a correspondence in 1974 which lasted until 1988. Their relationship, which was not sexual but one of mutual love, respect and support, was made more intense not just by their shared love of language and their experiences of racism and sexism, but by their both living with and going through cancer treatment.

Audre to Pat

Dear Pat,

I sit in this place to write you, wanting to do it in
my own hand but wanting also the clear precisions
of this machine that becomes like an excising filter,
sharp, inexorable. I love the way colored girls
always get the message – your call, after this letter
was framed and ready to jump out my eyes onto
some page. Between its intent and conception after
receiving yours, and the present now, has been, as
I told you, difficult days for me. But I am strong and
feisty and fighting all the way. Did a benefit reading
with Cheryl Clarke for a new lesbian magazine the
students at Hunter are starting for the University
as a whole and it gave me an enormous charge to
feel what such an event could mean just in terms of
change and the world's story and us, etc. and looking
at their wonderful young faces? I felt very blessed to
be who I am and where I was and a part of it all.

I have always loved you, Pat, and wanted for you
those things you wanted deeply for yourself. Do

not think me presumptuous – from the first time I met you in 1970 I knew that included your writing. I applaud your decision. I support you with my whole heart and extend myself to you in whatever way I can make this more possible for you. I hope you know by now I call your name whenever I can and will continue to do so. But you're right, you don't want to tie yourself up with so many gigs you don't have good solid time to stare at the walls and read the words stitched into the cracks between the nail holes.

Frances was still in Vermont when you were here and I was in NZ. She may be visiting too when I come up to SF in February, in which case we'll want a nice sound-proofed room with a big bed. Otherwise I will be real pleased to stay with you and Marty – I've been wanting to feel you and your family.

When I did not receive an answer to my letter last spring, I took a long and painful look at the 15 years we have known each other and decided that I had to accept the fact that we would never have the openness of friendship I always thought could be possible being the two strong Black women we are, with all our differences and sameness. Then your card from Nairobi, and I thought once again maybe when I'm out there next spring Pat and I will sit down once and for all and look at why we were not more available to each other all these years. I was overjoyed to get your letter and what it means in your life. There are conversations we need to have, Pat, each for her own clarity, and neither one of us has forever.

Things you must beware of right now –

A year seems like a lot of time now at this end – it isn't … Don't lose your sense of urgency on the one hand, on the other, don't be too hard on yourself – or expect too much.

Beware the terror of not producing.

Beware the urge to justify your decision.

Watch out for the kitchen sink and the plumbing and that painting that always needed being done. But remember that the body needs to create too.

Beware feeling you're not good enough to deserve it

Beware feeling you're too good to need it

Beware all the hatred you've stored up inside you, and the locks on your tender places.

Frances and I leave for Switzerland 12/14. If you write to me the address is

Prof. Audre Lorde

Lukas Klinik

CH-4144 Arlesheim

SWITZERLAND

I'll be there certainly until the 7th, probably until the 12th. I'd love to hear from you, and we will talk then. May this coming new year be a rich and fruitful one for you, Pat, and for those you love.

In the hand of Afrekete,

Love,

Audre

Pat to Audre

January 04, 1988

Dear Sister Love,

I have no idea where to begin this letter. There are
so many thoughts, and fears, and emotions moving
within me that I feel like a nuclear reactor out of
control. So, I am going to apologize up front for
the tone and content of this letter; not for what
I'm about to say, but simply because in a lot of
ways hearing this must be somewhat like being in
a relationship with someone a lot younger than
yourself. One can find oneself retracing a lot of
familiar ground [...] I brought you up to date on the
medical stuff so far on the phone [...] I've gotten
back most of the mobility in my arm and shoulder.
I must admit that I freaked out when I realized that
the motion was happening. The surgeon had told
me to exercise the arm and I did, but around day
four post-surgery, I couldn't stand to move it. Talk
about pain. Almost shocked me white. So, of course
I did what was so natural and stop moving the arm
altogether [...] So of course the next time I see the

surgeon, he's going 'hey you gotta move.' Now I
am probably the world's worst when it comes to
exercise. Like okay bore me to death. So I handled
the problem my way. You want Parker to move, put
a ball in the vicinity. So following my physician's
advice to take more pain medication and move
that arm, I returned to the gym and took more pain
medication and played racquetball. I lost all three
games, but I got the arm moving […] Now, you realize
that I am getting myself more frustrated. If I fully
accept my theory that anger is the primary cause
of having cancer then I must look around me and
make an assessment. Why am I angry? Who am I
angry at? And what can I do to change it? And of
course, the minute I start thinking along this vein, I
get even more angry. From the monumental thought
of overthrowing the system and ridding my life of
capitalism, racism, sexism, classism, to the smallest
nuisance […] Sister love, sister love, sister love. We
are not talking anything simple or easy here […] As
I told you on the phone, I was quite pleased to see
your article in *Essence*. One because these folks need
to be hearing from you chile and two because I got
to see this great photo of Diva Lorde in residence in
the islands […] Well love, I am about mid say down

page six. Still undone, but I'm tired and need to stop. Please answer this letter; I need to hear from you. I have some major concerns about what this will do to my relationship with my lover, but I'm too tired to get into this now.

Define 'processed foods'. Marty and I are debating milk and canned tomatoes. Take care. I love you.

Pat

Dear Sappho

The letters that follow come from a collection of that name, edited by Kay Turner and published in 1996, which contained over a hundred letters from lesbian lovers. We have a copy at Bishopsgate Institute, for anyone who wants to investigate further. The ones we have included here date from between 1985 and 1995 and are reprinted with kind permission of Thames & Hudson Ltd, London. After each letter there is more information supplied by the letter-writers themselves, which was up to date at the time of the publication of the first edition of the book.

Catherine to Cristina

November 1985

Darling,

I will continue on the path like a true warrior. I release you into the great sea of love from whence you first came to me. We will meet again. I love you eternally. I am committed to your soul forever.

You will never be farther from me than my heart, where you have a permanent resting place, free from fear, free from judgment.

I love you <u>unconditionally</u>, I am in your life to serve your soul. We have completed our first journey together in this lifetime. We have come together. We have infused each other with love and strength and wisdom. We have empowered one another, inspired and nurtured. You are very beloved to me, my precious wonder! I trust the future, I am excited to see what will happen next. I love living my vision. I let go of wanting you. I let go of my attachment to you.

I will miss holding you ... You are the most powerful lover I have ever had in this lifetime and

I surrendered to you completely with no fantasies other than of your energies merging and mingling with mine creating a cauldron of synergy out of which peace and justice is fed to the planet.

We have done some very good work together my darling comrade. The entire world has been uplifted by our partnership, by our love.

I have grown immeasurably with you and I see how far I still must go in this lifetime. So, I trust the future.

Love,

Your Catherine

In fact they roomed together at the Women's Conference in Beijing in September 1995.

Catherine and Cristina had roomed together at the Women's Conference in Beijing in September 1995, but at the time this letter was written they had just separated because Cristina was with someone else. After a period of readjustment, Catherine and Cristina resumed their very close friendship.

Stefanie to Judy

February 1985

Dear J,

Are you OK? I keep wondering, how could they do this? To threaten us. I hope it doesn't go any further. I'm so sorry about this. I just don't understand why – we aren't hurting anyone.

I just want to see you. I have to see you. Are you scared, baby? Me too. When we're together I feel safe. I want to make you feel safe.

Can you come tonight? Even if only for a short time. Even if you can't come alone.

Please try, please.

Love,
S.

Hi, it's me again. I came across this old letter today. In it I sounded so desperate. I needed to be with you so badly.

Remember when we used only initials in letters? We were so afraid someone would discover us. That all seems so long ago. At times though I still feel that same terror. The terror of misguided hatred.

Today, we are completely different people from those who found each other in high school.

How did we make it through? We've faced obstacles from the very beginning ... Why did we not just give up?

Maybe I had no other real option ... From deep down in my soul, I love you. With every part of me, I love you.

I sometimes feel that you are as essential to my survival as air and water. It's as if my real life began ten years ago. I awoke to the bright sunshine after a dark frightening dream.

You are my happiness, my music, my laughter. Thank you for this life.

Happy tenth, angel.

Love, S

As Stefanie wrote to *Dear Sappho*'s editor, 'I found the womon [*sic*] of my dreams in high school. We thought we were straight. We've loved each other through harassment, illness, poverty, and self-doubt. In May 1995, we celebrated our 10th year together.'

Laura to Madisson

7.19.93, 11.30 a.m.

Madisson, Madisson, Madisson

I am obsessed with you. I can't eat. I can't sleep.
I only can think of you and our love-making on
Friday night. Thoughts of you crying – thinking of
how beautiful I find you. Being scared to let me kiss
you everywhere – afraid to be so totally vulnerable
… I want to possess you, capture you, belong to
you. Belong to you – belong to you – belong to you.
Madisson, I belong to you. I surrender my body, my
heart, my soul to you, my beautiful Madisson.

I am more afraid than I have ever been in my life.
Afraid of the totality of my desire for you. Afraid
you'll ask me to leave Terry, afraid you won't ask

me to leave Terry. What's going to happen to me? ...
How can I live without you now that I've found you?
I cannot ...

Come to my house on our next weekday off
and spend the day with me. Start in the morning,
make love, go on a picnic, hold hands, tell me your
dreams, make love again and again and again ... Let
me court you, woo you, seduce you ... Let me rub
our wetness together. This time I won't hold back
my climax. I love your hands, lips, pelvis, legs ....
I love you, angel. I love you Madisson forever and
without conditions or hesitation. If you reject me
now – I will die.

Laura

In 1995 Laura told *Dear Sappho*'s editor, '[W]e've been together two years now. Madisson is very androgynous and I am very femme. I did leave Terry (my partner of 10 years) about two weeks after this letter was written.'

'Black men loving Black men is the revolutionary act of the eighties.'

Joseph Beam was a gay rights activist and author of colour who worked to achieve greater acceptance of gay life in the Black community in the US in the 1980s. Born in Philadelphia, he attended Franklin College in Indiana, where he was influenced by the Civil Rights and the Black Power movements and was active in college journalism. Beam became well acquainted with local and national gay figures and institutions while employed at Giovanni's Room, a bookstore in Philadelphia's Center City District and one of the main contact points for lesbians and gays in the city in the early 1980s. His articles and short stories appeared in numerous gay newspapers and magazines, including *Au Courant*, *Blackheart*, *The Advocate* and *New York Native*. The Lesbian and Gay Press Association gave him an award for outstanding achievement by a minority journalist in 1984. He joined the Executive Committee of the National Coalition of Black Lesbians and Gays in 1985, becoming editor of their new journal, *Black/Out*. *In the Life*, an anthology of writings by and about gay men of colour edited by Beam, features a piece he wrote entitled 'Brother to Brother: Words from the Heart', which speaks movingly about being Black and gay in America in the 1980s. Beam was working on a sequel to *In the Life* at the time of his death from HIV-related disease in 1988. The book was completed by his mother, Dorothy, and the gay poet Essex Hemphill, and published under the title *Brother to Brother* in 1991.

Rebel Dykes

The 2021 documentary *Rebel Dykes* shows what happens when 'punk met feminism, told through the lives of a gang of lesbians in the riotous London of the 1980s'. The women now known as Rebel Dykes describe themselves as part of 'a radical scene: squatters, BDSM nightclubs, anti-Thatcher rallies, protests demanding action around AIDS and the fierce ties of chosen family ... made up of young punk women on the edge of society. As a movement they were heavily involved in art and culture, creating bands, art, club nights, zines and festivals.' The following letter and poem, housed at Bishopsgate Institute, are from one Rebel Dyke to another.

... to Jane from M

16/4/94

16:55

On Easter Sunday – what was going through my
mind is to wake up before you make breakfast &
bring it up to you with a surprise of wearing my
waiters jacket but an extra special as it's Easter being
a bunny at the same time. I wanted to be your Easter
Bunny. Wearing Bunny ears, white bow-tie & not
forgetting white fluffy tail. What do you do? today
of all days: we woke-up. you go down for a while
& come up with the breakfast tray & Easter Egg.
Of all days when I wanted to surprise you. I was
gutted. In tears. You spoiled my surprise. Oh No I
was thinking. You tried to calm my down by saying
'it's okay you can do launch' but it's not the same. It
wasn't long, well about 1700 we were hungry again.
'Okay I'm going to make you breakfast properly,
Where's the legging for my outfit'. It was down stairs
because you have done the washing, so you knew
that I'm going to wear my outfit but not everything
else. Downstairs in the Kitchen Afra helped me to

put on my tail. She taught I looked quite. I couldn't wait. Breakfast ready I look like a bunny now. I went to see Bea just to make sure I looked alright. She said I look sweet, so I said to come with me because I didn't have my glasses on me & I need to see your expression so she could see it & tell me. Oh Jane I was dying to see the expression on your face.

'Knock, Knock'. 'Come In'.

I open the door, your sitting on the bed, under the covers. You were looking down thinking this is just another breakfast.

'Your breakfast is served Ma'am' you look up, your eyes lights. Your face 'Oh' loudly 'You look beautiful' God I love that expression on your face. I wiggled my tail just like a bunny. I hope you liked my surprise. & an Easter to remember. Well not quietly.

Not after you fell asleep and ½ E we took later on, while I was rushing with my Bunny outfit.

HAPPY EASTER JANE x

She is laying next to me

Her hips on mine

Her hands on me

Moving slowly

Gentle is how it feel

Covering my chest

Moving across it

She finds it

Her fingers on it

She is generating electricity

Holding it with two fingers

Gently she shakes the world

Shocks are travelling

Hips are moving

Thrusting tongues

Left hand moving down

Till she finds it

The steam

The sea gushing

For her touch

Hungry for her thrust

Two In

Moving deep

Moving fast
She knows is not enough
My hand on her
Three Four Five
Pushed in
I'm all yours
Touch me deep
I'm Wild
Tribal is how I dance
Madness is our common
She is all inside
Grab me
Deep inside is how I feel
I'm all yours
She possesses all my powers
My eyes are closed
The sky opens
She guides me
She shows me the World beyond
Her World
She is the Queen
She is taken me
I'm hers
No demands

No resistance
A light shines on my eyes
Light generating from her
She owns me
I'm a slave to her desires
On my knees
I'm at her feet
She holds my face
Looks into my eyes
I drown
I drown in her blue sky

MY QUEEN
YOU ARE MY KINGDOM

Tears drop from my eyes
Into the sea
The sea is high
My heart beat are fast
My soul leaves me
I'm just a body
With her touch
She revives me
Open my eyes
I look at her

I cry

No control

Don't go

Don't leave

Dear Me

Back in 2009, Joseph Galliano – co-founder and CEO of Queer Britain, the national LGBTQ+ museum – hit upon the idea of publishing a collection of letters written by notable people to their sixteen-year-old selves. By turns moving, heartfelt, hilarious and inspiring, it includes letters from Stephen Fry, Mark Gatiss and Pam St Clement, among many others, and makes a fantastic read, providing insight into the letter-writers' lives, both at the time of writing and when they were trembling on the brink of adulthood.

Paul Swing
(b.1962)

Born in Canada, Paul Swing is a writer who has lived in the UK since 1985 and volunteered with Switchboard (formerly London Lesbian & Gay Switchboard) helpline for many years. His memoirs of life as a gay man in London from the 1980s to the present day are held at Bishopsgate Institute.

He wrote the following on the back of a birthday card sent to his then boyfriend:

Wed, January 15/88

Shahin;

I wish you every happiness on this, your coming of age.

I never thought of sleeping with you as being an illegal act until now. –

I loved the Saturday night we had after Michael Clark: I've never been more honest. I think I let myself be loved that night – I'm glad it was with you.

I will always think of the experience of that night in my room as one of the best in my life. Happy Birthday!!

all my love, Paul xo

And this was the inscription at the front of a book given to Paul by an ex-lover when Paul broke up with him:

The last time we met you were telling me of being infatuated. I hated every word you said. But infatuation is a strange face I know too well. There was nothing I could say, so I left trying to smile and trying not to look hurt.

I am giving this book to you, which as you know is one of my favourites. Hearing you speaking about what I love the most was unreal – x Fabio

Finally, in Paul's own words, 'This is a message I wrote on a paper towel and left on the floor in Norman's bedroom for him to find the next morning. This was about a month before he died [in 2019]. He [the artist Norman Caleb Riseley] was my partner for 12 years and best friend for over 30, and I was caring for him while he was dying of cancer.'

Saying:
'I love you!'
doesn't even
come close
to it.
Always,
Paul x

Shaun Dellenty
(b.1968)

Shaun Dellenty is an educator and activist whose internationally celebrated, multi-award-winning teacher training strategy has been facilitating LGBTQ+ inclusion within learning communities since 2009.

Shaun trained as a primary school teacher while also working as a presenter, corporate host, actor and stand-up comedian. In late 2009 his school carried out surveys with primary-aged pupils. The data revealed that 75 per cent of them were experiencing homophobic bullying on a daily basis, regardless of whether they identified as LGBTQ+ or not. The homophobia was targeted at any child who simply didn't fit perceived social 'norms'. Shaun decided to come out as gay to the whole school community in an assembly. He then wrote a compassionate LGBTQ+ teacher-training strategy called 'Inclusion for All', aimed initially at primary schools and subsequently for faith and secondary schools and teacher-training faculties. Having delivered it with great success at his own school first, over the next ten years he went on to roll it out to over 65,000 UK educators. National and international organizations including Stonewall, Amnesty International, the Church of England, Kidscape, Show Racism the Red Card, the NSPCC, teaching trade unions and politicians worked with Shaun to develop their own LGBTQ+ inclusion programmes.

In 2016 Shaun was awarded the Mayor of Southwark's highest civic honour at Southwark Cathedral, receiving the Freedom of Southwark, was named 'Education Champion 2016' at the national Excellence in Diversity awards, and was presented with a Points of Light award by the prime minister for services to education and LGBTQ+ communities.

That same year one of Shaun's former students wrote the following letter to him on his website.

Hi, not an enquiry just a message; I left Alfred Salter Primary School in 2011 after being there since 2005 and I have so much to thank the school and you in particular for; I found Alfred Salter such a happy and friendly place to be and after discovering that I myself fall on the LGBTQ+ spectrum, I believe without doubt that the self acceptance I felt was as a result of the inclusive and loving environment that was fostered at Alfred Salter. I was never taught or in an environment where sexualities were discriminated against and I therefore never felt any of this towards myself and I can't thank you or any of the teachers enough for this. Only after leaving Alfred Salter did I realise how uniquely brilliant it was; none of my peers now have been exposed to such diversity in terms of religion, race, special needs and sexuality, and I can't tell you how much all of these things have shaped me into the liberal person that I'm proud to be now, so thank you. I still remember the assembly in which you came out in, it made such an impact on me; when I discovered your website I had to reach out and thank you, you are what teachers are supposed to be. Thank you.

A Prize-winning Proposal

The investigative journalist Ronan Farrow's amazing Pulitzer Prize-winning book *Catch and Kill* (2019) details his years-long struggle to hold Harvey Weinstein to account for his abuse and exploitation of women actors over more than twenty years in Hollywood. In exposing Weinstein and other men in power, Farrow and his journalistic colleagues at *The New Yorker* set in motion events that would spawn the #MeToo and Time's Up movements. Working on the book, Farrow's partner Jon Lovett – a former speechwriter for Barack Obama and co-founder, with Jon Favreau and Tommy Vietor, of Crooked Media, whose output includes the excellent podcasts *Pod Save America*, *Lovett or Leave It* and *America Dissected* – would help out by reading early drafts of the manuscript of *Catch and Kill*. In one such draft, Farrow inserted a proposal: 'Marriage?' As Farrow writes, 'He [Lovett] read the draft, and found the proposal here, and said "Sure."'

MC Sherman
(b.1999)

MC Sherman has written the following introduction to their letters:

MC Sherman is a queer college student who is studying English with a minor in Religious Studies. They are pursuing a lifestyle of being a fiction writer and poet besides their unknown professional career. When not writing or taking classes, they are outside or reading in various locations.

About the letters
The letters were written to the subject who, after some consideration, became my first love. They were written as a form of therapy for my nervous and stressed-out thoughts. Especially since my previous experiences with queer relationships didn't turn out to what I was expecting; I was severely unprepared in high school. Writing the letters helped me sort out my thoughts and work on creating a close friendship with the subject.

The context of the letters

It all started around the time I had realized I had a crush on the person. They worked on the same military base as I did and I had known this person for quite some time before the butterflies decided to set in. However, the feeling of it gave me conflicting feelings. The months were leading up to the infamous 2020 American election and I was nervous about my safety in the small, seemingly red town. That was terrifying to me as a queer person and having a crush on someone was, in my opinion at the time, unneeded. But at the same time, I found myself wanting to be with this person, even if everything turned out for the worst. I had decided to write the letters as a way to cope with them. However, after gaining some courage, I was able to talk to the person about coming over for dinner and such. To this day, we are decent friends and I am still working out the nerve to tell them how I feel.

Dear J—, I wish it wasn't like this, but for some reason, I really care about you. I don't know why, though. Out of everyone who I see on a daily basis, you just stuck with me. All you did was come into the store and the next thing I knew, I felt the familiar flip in my stomach. Affection, admiration, love, I don't know. But I wish it didn't happen.

I'm barely an adult and still in college. It feels weird to see you and have some kind of feeling in my stomach. And there are other parts of me that I'm too scared to admit to anyone. I don't want any of this to be known.

But at this point, I really care about you. It feels alcoholic, like the bubbly and warm feeling I would get from light cocktails. I like the feeling, despite the fact that I'm sure no one else I know would take this yearning lightly. Sure, I'm surrounded by similar relationships, but I'm not sure how they'll react to my news. I don't have much to fall back on, so pretending that I don't have any interest in you is more of a survival tactic. Don't take it personally, it's just how I learned to live in society. But it's not easy for me, though.

I feel like the emotions (maybe I should just call them affections) are eating me alive. And there is also the familiar tinge of pain; you are an unrequited heartbreak I need to deal with alone.

MC

10/31/20

Dear J—,

The heartache feels better now, but I still feel the usual knots and butterflies whenever I see you. The only time it hurts is when I'm reminded that you won't be here for long. Two people I was already starting to become friends with have left because of the Coast Guard. It hurts to think that I could waste another opportunity of telling someone how I feel.

But I don't know what's keeping me back. Possibly the fear of rejection. Or the fact that I might not be the best-suited partner for you. I'm loud, nervous, forgetful of tasks, and I have a tendency of putting other people before me. And that trait is only positive until it reaches its limit, which is where I am heading. While I am working on these flaws and getting better, you deserve someone who is more mature. You seem to be into a more quiet form of love. I do, as well, but I need more time.

At least I can say that this love isn't as painful as it was before. Now it's a matter of whether I can break through the remainder of my shell.

Here's to hoping,

M

11/3/21

Dear J—,

It's unfortunately election night. To escape the updates, I've been staying in my room, hoping not to hear my family's opinion on the matter. So far, it seems to be good, but I am nervous about it. Even though I voted, I'm worried about the state of things in the country. Especially since I'm a person who was born a woman but now identifies differently and prefers the company of different people. I guess I just confessed to you. I'm queer.

Even though my family says that they love me (or they act like they do), I'm scared of what they'll say. Specifically, I'm scared about what they truly think about me and the thousands of others who had to deal with the hate and crushing laws for four years. I've been preparing myself for bias and hate, possibly even rejection. But rejection from someone you love is difficult to comprehend.

Maybe that's the reason why I'm so afraid of confessing my affections to you. What would you do if I told you?

All I know is that I just want to be with you right now. Together on the couch or on the bed, nothing has to be playing. I would prefer to avoid the election and maybe binge a TV series with you instead. Thinking of that now made me think about how I'd rather be with you in any situation. The world could be on fire or collapsing and I wouldn't care. Sappy, but true. You make me feel like I can through the chaos of our time.

Take care of yourself.

MC

Ivan Nuru
(b.1999)

Ivan Nuru is a Black American poet, from Mississippi. His first project is a self-published poetry chapbook titled *You're So Patient with Me*. He is currently working on his debut full-length poetry collection.

November 2021

Dad,

It's okay. It's more than okay – it's beautiful.
That's what I wanted to say the other day
when you were giving your lover a massage,
but stopped when you caught me looking.
My apologies for not saying it I know
you needed to hear that. You never
talk about what it's like being an older Black
gay man, and I'm so curious as your gay son.
There have been so many moments like the other day,
when I startled you, because you're not used
to anyone seeing you be soft and in love.
I know that fear has reached places inside of
us that love has yet catch up to, but the thing I'm curious
about is how are we going to help love get there.
I know it won't be the silence we held onto all these years.
I used to resent you for not having answers
to all my questions growing up as a Black gay kid.
The older I got, the more I understand that
you may have more questions than me.
Someday I hope we can stop being so

The Love That Dares

afraid of each other and what makes us
beautiful Black gay men. I haven't read a story
like ours because it hasn't been written yet,
so I thought I'd start with this letter.
I thought I'd start by saying, it's okay.

Love,
Your son

Acknowledgements

We would like to express our eternal gratitude to the following people for their help and support in putting this book together:

Ellie Corbett, Ellen Sandford O'Neill, Ben Gardiner and Rachel Silverlight at Octopus/Ilex.
Copy-editor Lesley Levene for her keen eye and patience; proofreader Robert Anderson and indexer Helen Snaith.
Our friends and colleagues at Bishopsgate Institute, especially Stef Dickers and Colleen Goldspink
Cheryl Bailey and the team at Sheffield City Archives
Chris Hilton and all at Britten Pears Arts
Laura Kuhn, Julie Enszer and Phyllis Armstrong
Shaun Dellenty
MC Sherman
Paul Swing

References & Resources

Here is just a small sample of some of the amazing books, articles, websites and podcasts we've discovered while researching this book. If you want to learn more about the lives and times of any of the letter-writers quoted in this book, do check them out. Many are available to read at Bishopsgate Institute Special Collections and Archives.

Archives

Susan B. Anthony Papers: Correspondence, 1905;
Bound volume. 1905, 1846. Manuscript/Mixed
Material. https://www.loc.gov/item/mss11049001/.

'Roles and priorities', archived 18 November 2012 at
the Wayback Machine, the Archbishop of Canterbury's
official website

The Authors League Fund and St Bride's Church, as
joint literary executors of the Estate of Djuna Barnes

Katharine Lee Bates Papers (3P-Bates), Wellesley
College Archives

John Dalby Archive, Bishopsgate Institute

Shaun Dellenty Archive, Bishopsgate Institute

Eva Palmer to Natalie Barney; Dolly Wilde to Natalie
Barney: The Bibliothèque Littéraire Jacques Doucet; Paris,
France

Radclyffe Hall and Una Vincenzo, Lady Troubridge, Papers (Manuscript Collection MS-01793). Harry Ransom Center, The University of Texas at Austin

Rebel Dykes Archive, Bishopsgate Institute

Siegfried Sassoon, George Merrill and Edward Carpenter letters: Sheffield City Archives (Carpenter Collection MSS.363-11, MSS.363-12, MSS.363-17)

Elizabeth Wade White papers, Manuscripts and Archives Division, The New York Public Library

West Yorkshire Archive Service, Calderdale; SH:7/ ML/E/15

Walt Whitman letter to Henry Stafford: Whitman Archive [ID: loc.03996]

The Charles E. Feinberg Collection of the Papers of Walt Whitman, 1839–1919, Library of Congress, Washington, DC

Oscar Wilde letter to Walt Whitman: Whitman Archive (ID: loc.04865)

Books

Akrigg, G. P. V., *Letters of King James VI & I*
(University of California Press, 1984)

Anselm of Canterbury, *Cur deus homo* (Griffith,
Farran, Okeden & Welsh, 1889)

Beam, Joseph (ed.), *In the Life: A Black Gay Anthology*
(Alyson Publications, 1996; repr. Redbone Press, 2008)

Bolt, Rodney, *As Good as God, As Clever as the Devil:
The Impossible Life of Mary Benson* (Atlantic Books,
2011)

Bordin, Ruth, and Birgitta Anderson, *Alice Freeman
Palmer: The Evolution of a New Woman* (University of
Michigan Press, 1993)

Bridcut, John, *Britten's Children* (Faber & Faber, 2006)

Bucknell, Katherine, *The Animals: Love Letters
between Christopher Isherwood and Don Bachardy*
(Farrar, Straus and Giroux, 2014)

Dellenty, Shaun, *Celebrating Difference* (Bloomsbury Education, 2019)

Dyer, Terry, *Letters to a Gay Black Boy* (independently published, 2020)

Enszer, Julie (ed.), *Sister Love: The Letters of Audre Lorde and Pat Parker, 1974–1989* (A Midsummer Night's Press & Sinister Wisdom, 2018)

Faderman, Lillian, *Surpassing the Love of Men: Romantic Friendship and Love between Women from the Renaissance to the Present* (William Morrow, 1981)

Faderman, Lillian, *Odd Girls and Twilight Lovers* (Columbia University Press, 1991)
Galliano, Joseph (ed.), *Dear Me: A Letter to My Sixteen-Year-Old Self* (Simon & Schuster, 2009)

Gerson, Noel B., *George Sand: A Biography of the First Modern, Liberated Woman* (Hale, 1973)
Glasgow, Joanne, *Your John: The Love Letters of Radclyffe Hall* (NYU Press, 1999)

Haines, C.R. (ed.), *The Correspondence of Marcus Cornelius Fronto* (2 vols, William Heinemann, 1919)

Haring Judd, Peter, *The Akeing Heart: Letters between Sylvia Townsend Warner, Valentine Ackland and Elizabeth Wade White* (Handheld Press, 2018)

Hickok, Lorena A., *Eleanor Roosevelt: Reluctant First Lady* (Dodd Mead, 1980)

Johnson, Thomas and Theodora Van Wagenen Ward, *The Letters of Emily Dickinson* (Harvard University Press, 1958)

Judd, Peter Haring *The Akeing Heart: Letters between Sylvia Townsend Warner, Valentine Ackland and Elizabeth Wade White* (Handheld Press, 2018)

Kuhn, Laura (ed.), *Love, Icebox: Letters from John Cage to Merce Cunningham* (The John Cage Trust, 2019)

Lapsley, Hilary, *Margaret Mead and Ruth Benedict: The Kinship of Women* (University of Massachusetts Press, 1999)

Liddington, Jill, *Presenting the Past: Anne Lister of Halifax (1791–1840)* (Pennine Pens, 1994)

Long, Michael G, *I Must Resist: Bayard Rustin's life in Letters* (City Lights Books, 2012)

Mavor, Elizabeth, *The Ladies of Llangollen: A Study in Romantic Friendship* (Penguin, 1971; repr. 1974)

Modell, Judith Schachter, *Ruth Benedict: Patterns of a Life* (University of Pennsylvania Press, 1983)

Norton, Rictor, *My Dear Boy: Gay Love Letters throughout the Centuries* (Leyland Publications, 1998)

O'Hara, John Myers (trans.), *The Poems of Sappho: An Interpretative Rendition into English* (Project Gutenberg, 2013)

Pollak, Vivian R., *The Erotic Whitman* (University of California Press, 2000)
Popova, Maria, *Figurings* (Ballantine Books, 2019)

Schenkar, Joan, *Truly Wilde: The Unsettling Story of Dolly Wilde, Oscar's Unusual Niece* (Basic Books, 2000)

Sharpe, Kevin M., *Remapping Early Modern England: The Culture of Seventeenth-century England* (Cambridge University Press, 2000)

Smith, Martha Nell, 'Susan and Emily Dickinson, Their Lives, in Letters', in Wendy Martin (ed.), *The Cambridge Companion to Emily Dickinson* (Cambridge University Press, 2002)

Smyth, Ethel, *As Time Went On* (Longmans, 1936)

Souhami, Diana, *Gluck* (Quercus, 1988)

Souhami, Diana, *Mrs Keppel and Her Daughter* (Quercus, 1996)

Souhami, Diana, *Trials of Radclyffe Hall* (Quercus, 1998)

Souhami, Diana, *Natalie and Romaine* (Quercus, 2004)

Souhami, Diana, *No Modernism without Lesbians* (Head of Zeus, 2020)

Streitmatter, Roger (ed.), *Empty without You: The*

Intimate Letters of Eleanor Roosevelt and Lorena Hickok (Da Capo Press, 2000)

Stroeher, Vicki P., Clark, Nicholas and Brimmer, Jude (eds), *My Beloved Man: The Letters of Benjamin Britten and Peter Pears* (The Boydell Press, 2016)

Sturgis, Matthew, *Oscar: A Life* (Head of Zeus, 2018)

Taylor, Verta, Whittier, Nancy and Rupp, Leila J., *Feminist Frontiers* (8th edn; McGraw Hill, 2008)

Turner, Kay, *Dear Sappho: A Legacy of Lesbian Love Letters* (Thames & Hudson, 1996)

Vaid-Menon, Alok, *Beyond the Gender Binary* (Penguin, 2020)

Whitbread, Helena (ed.), *No Priest but Love: Excerpts from the Diaries of Anne Lister, 1824–1826* (Dalesman Publishing Co., 1992)

Articles

Djuna Barnes *et al.*, 'The Letters of Djuna Barnes and Emily Holmes Coleman (1935–1936)', *Missouri Review*, Vol. 22, No. 3 (1999), pp. 105–46. Project MUSE, doi:10.1353/mis.1999.0013

Brideoake, Fiona, '"Extraordinary Female Affection": The Ladies of Llangollen and the Endurance of Queer Community', *Romanticism on the Net*, Issue 36–37, November 2004

Daughters of Bilitis, *The Ladder*

Schwarz, Judith, '"Yellow Clover": Katharine Lee Bates and Katharine Coman', *Frontiers: A Journal of Women Studies*, Vol. 4, No. 1, Spring 1979

https://etheses.whiterose.ac.uk/2471/1/DX190733.pdf

https://www.rebeldykes1980s.com

'To My Excellent Lucasia, on Our Friendship', Katherine Philips, https://www.poetryfoundation.org/poems/50445/to-my-excellent-lucasia-on-our-friendship

Websites

https://www.theallusionist.org/bequest
https://www.autostraddle.com
https://www.thelogbooks.org
https://www.themarginalian.org
https://www.poz.com/blog/
love-letter-black-gay-men-early-hiv-movement
https://www.rictornorton.co.uk – a treasure trove of
essays on 'Gay History & Literature' by Rictor Norton
https://scalawagmagazine.org/2020/05/
black-gay-hiv-aids/
https://www.sfwp.com/quarterly/a-love-letter-to-my-
gay-black-brother-andre-alexander-lancaster
https://www.takatapui.nz – a resource hub for
Takatāpui and their Whānau
https://www.wqxr.org/story/
musical-love-letters-dedications-lgbt-composers

Podcasts

The Allusionist
Bad Gays
Homo Sapiens
Making Gay History
The Log Books
Lovett or Leave It
Queersplaining
The Animals: A Love Story Told in Letters

Index

Credits

The authors and publisher would like to thank the following individuals and institutions for their kind permission to reproduce the letters in this book.

Copies of most of the books cited are held and can be consulted at Bishopsgate Institute's Special Collections and Archives.

Anne Lister & Ann Walker:
West Yorkshire Archive Service, Calderdale; SH:7/
ML/E/15

George Sand:
Translation by Ellie Corbett, © Octopus Publishing
Group

Emily Dickinson:
THE LETTERS OF EMILY DICKINSON, edited by
Thomas H. Johnson, Associate Editor, Theodora Ward,
Cambridge, Mass.: The Belknap Press of Harvard
University Press, Copyright © 1958 by the President
and Fellows of Harvard College. Copyright © renewed
1986 by the President and Fellows of Harvard College.
Copyright © 1914, 1924, 1932, 1942 by Martha
Dickinson Bianchi. Copyright © 1952 by Alfred Leete
Hampson. Copyright © 1960 by Mary L. Hampson.
Used by permission. All rights reserved.

Susan B Anthony & Anna Dickinson:
Anthony, Susan B. Susan B. Anthony Papers:
Correspondence, -1905; Bound volume. - 1905, 1846.
Manuscript/Mixed Material. https://www.loc.gov/item/
mss11049001/.

Oscar Wilde:

The Charles E. Feinberg Collection of the Papers of
Walt Whitman, 1839–1919, Library of Congress,
Washington, D.C.

Walt Whitman:

The Charles E. Feinberg Collection of the Papers of
Walt Whitman, 1839–1919, Library of Congress,
Washington, D.C.

Katharine Lee Bates:

Katharine Lee Bates Papers, (3P-Bates), Wellesley
College Archives

Edward Carpenter and George Merrill:
Edward Carpenter Archive, Sheffield City Archives

Siegfried Sassoon:
Edward Carpenter Archive, Sheffield City Archives

Vita Sackville West:
Reproduced with permission of Curtis Brown Group
Ltd, London on behalf of The Beneficiaries of the Estate
of Vita Sackville West. Copyright © Vita Sackville West

Dolly Wilde:
With the kind permission of the Bibliothèque Littéraire
Jacques Doucet, Chancellerie des universités de Paris

Radclyffe/John Hall:
Radclyffe Hall and Una Vincenzo, Lady Troubridge
Papers (Manuscript Collection MS-01793). Harry
Ransom Center, The University of Texas at Austin

Djuna Barnes:
The Authors League Fund and St. Bride's Church,
as joint literary executors of the Estate of Djuna Barnes

Gluck:
Reproduced with the kind permission of Penny Gluckstein

Sylvia Townsend Warner & Valentine Ackland:
The Estate of Sylvia Townsend Warner and
Valentine Ackland

Benjamin Britten & Peter Pears:
Chris Hilton/Britten Pears Arts

John Cage:
Laura Kuhn/John Cage Trust

Dear Sappho letters:
From *Dear Sappho: A Legacy of Lesbian Love Letters* edited by Kay Turner, © 1996, published in the UK by Thames & Hudson Ltd. U.S. edition, *Between Us: A Legacy of Lesbian Love Letters*, published by Chronicle Books. Reprinted by kind permission of Thames & Hudson Ltd., London

Rebel Dykes:
Rebel Dykes Archive, Bishopsgate Institute

Paul Swing:
Courtesy of Paul Swing, Bishopsgate Institute Special Collections and Archives ref

Shaun Dellenty:
Shaun Dellenty Archive, Bishopsgate Institute

MC Sherman:
courtesy of MC Sherman/personal correspondence with Barbara Vesey at Bishopsgate Institute

Ivan Nuru:
Used by kind permission of Ivan Nuru

A note on the photographs

Robert Workman is a photographer who worked for *Gay News* for over ten years. Having left his native Scotland in 1965 to study architecture in London, after a stint as agent-manager for some friends and their band Gas Works, he received an unexpected windfall in the shape of £500 left to him by an uncle. He came out to his friends, bought a Hasselblad – the camera of choice for contemporary fashion photographers David Bailey, Dufy and Terence Donovan – taught himself to develop film and make prints, and began a notable and very successful career. He photographed gay life as lived at the Coleherne and The Catacombs; he covered the annual Campaign for Homosexual Equality conference for *Gay News* as a freelance photographer. His idea for an article on gay street names (Great Queen Street, Mincing Lane, Dyke Road, etc.) became a long-running feature; his 'Scene and Heard' series recorded the sights and sounds of public demonstrations, Tricky Dicky discos, Sappho meetings, gay outdoor clubs, biking groups, events, festivals, celebrities and even the gay nude beach at Shell Bay.

Images featured on the cover and endpapers of this book courtesy of the Robert Workman Archive, Bishopsgate Institute

BISHOPSGATE INSTITUTE

Dear Reader,

Thank you for reading, but our work is not yet finished. Our narrative can only continue with you to help tell the story of LGBTQ+ love for future generations.

We would be privileged and honoured to house your love letters in perpetuity as part of the Love That Dares Archive in the Special Collections at Bishopsgate Institute.

Any interested parties please email Library@ Bishopsgate.org.uk

Love,
The Future

First published in the United
Kingdom in 2022 by Ilex, an imprint
of Octopus Publishing Group Ltd
Carmelite House
50 Victoria Embankment
London EC4Y 0DZ
www.octopusbooks.co.uk
www.octopusbooksusa.com

An Hachette UK Company
www.hachette.co.uk

Distributed in the US by
Hachette Book Group
1290 Avenue of the Americas,
4th and 5th Floors
New York, NY 10104

Distributed in Canada by
Canadian Manda Group
664 Annette St., Toronto,
Ontario, Canada M6S 2C8

ISBN 978-1-78157-829-2

A CIP catalogue record for this book
is available from the British Library.

Printed and bound in the United
Kingdom.

10 9 8 7 6 5 4 3 2 1

Publisher: Alison Starling
Commissioning Editor: Ellie Corbett
Managing Editor: Rachel Silverlight
Assistant Editor:
Ellen Sandford O'Neill
Art Director: Ben Gardiner
Typeset by Jeremy Tilston
Production Manager: Caroline Alberti

This FSC® label means that materials
used for the product have been
responsibly sourced.